REJECTION LETTERS OF BOOK AGENTS

WITH COMMENTS

BY MILA ILKOVA

M

New York

REJECTION LETTERS OF BOOK AGENTS
© 2023 by Mila Ilkova
Design © 2023 by Mila Ilkova
ISBN 979-8-9877558-7-7
Library of Congress Control Number: 2023907908

What most writers go through.
The ones that don't are dead.
It'd be hilarious if this book became a bestseller.

1

Thank you for your interest in working with the agents of Aragi Inc. We're very sorry to be sending this letter but on the basis of your query, we're afraid we can't consider your work. The high volume of submissions we receive forces us to be extremely selective, and we don't believe we'll be able to give your work the time and attention it deserves.

We wish you the best of luck in your search for representation.

Sincerely,
Aragi Inc.

That's fine. I was expecting a few rejections at first. Agents have their lists, and publishers have their lists, and sometimes they just don't match with the writer's creativity. It's a very subjective industry, I know.

Thank you for thinking of me with your query for TEN MYRIAD MOVES. While this sounds like a strong project, I'm afraid it doesn't strike me as a likely fit with me and my particular editorial contacts.

I wish you well in finding the right agent for your work.

Anne Hawkins
John Hawkins & Associates, Inc.
80 Maiden Lane - Suite 1503
New York, New York 10038

Don't be afraid — the novel is not that scary.

Dear Author:

Thank you. We have received your query.

Because of the high volume of email submissions we receive, we will only get in touch with you if we are interested in your project; if we are interested in your work, we will be in touch within six to eight weeks.

Thank you.

The Irene Goodman Literary Agency

What if I wrote that to agents? "The number of agents I'm simultaneously querying can't let me write personalized emails. But your work is very important to me, so don't get discouraged."

Thank you for emailing The Bindery Agency.

We're committed to reading every submission, including yours. If you included all of the relevant information about your project, including sample content, we will determine whether or not it fits our current needs and interests within 8-10 weeks. If it fits our current needs, someone will reach out to you and request more information.

Warm regards,
The Bindery

*Sign up for our monthly email newsletter today at www.TheBinderyAgency.com <http://www.thebinderyagency.com/> and receive our FREE Book Proposal Template. You'll also discover articles and ebooks full of writing tips and publishing advice.

Our new podcast, "On Publishing" features interviews with experts from the world of publishing (listen now at our website or at https://anchor.fm/onpublishingpodcast.

Or instead of blogging and podcasting, you could do... um... agenting. And help with a writer's career like you all claim you do.

5

Dear Mila –

Many thanks for writing. You have an interesting story to tell and there's a lot to like
about your approach. But in the end I'm afraid
I didn't come away quite fully convinced this
was something I think I'd be able to represent
successfully. I'm sorry not to be more enthusiastic but thanks nonetheless for giving me a
chance to review it and best of luck in finding
it the right home.

Best,
Farley

--

Chase Literary Agency
11 Broadway, Suite 1010
New York, NY 10004
212-477-5100 -|- chaseliterary.com

With Harvey Weinstein in the film
industry, women at least knew
whose dick to suck if they wanted
an Oscar. There is no such thing
in the literary world.

Thank you for your interest in querying Browne & Miller Literary Associates about your book project. **However, we are currently closed to queries.** We will update our website when the inbox has re-opened, and invite you to try us again then.

Browne & Miller does **NOT** represent: children's books including Young Adult and Middle Grade fiction; sci-fi, fantasy, or horror novels; poetry; short stories; screenplays; memoirs; previously published titles/series; novellas or academic works. For more information on the types of projects we will be seeking in 2022, please visit: www.publishersmarketplace.com/members/mpdinc/

Yeah, like I'll remember who to query again after 200 personalized emails.

1

Dear Mila,

Thank you for sending me your query for TEN MYRIAD MOVES. As I am not sure your project is the right fit for my list at this time, I will regretfully have to pass. Thank you for considering me, and I wish you the best of luck with your future queries.

Sincerely,
Jess Regel

Coffee. I need more coffee. I wonder how many types of milk exist in the world. Do they only milk nuts, cows, and goats or is there anything else? Stop it, Mila! Concentrate on what's important — bothering strangers over email and hearing back how afraid they are.

8

Dear Mila,
Thank you for your query.
While TEN MYRIAD MOVES sounds interesting, I'm afraid it's not right for my list at this time. I appreciate your email and wish you luck finding an agent who can successfully champion your work.
Best,
Kevan Lyon

Nipple milk...sounds very perv. Nonfat nipple milk grande latte, please! Oh, boy...we might be able to order blowjobs at Starbucks soon, just like in Idiocracy movie.

Dear Mila,

Thank you very much for your query, which we have read with interest. Unfortunately, the project does not seem right for this agency, and we are sorry that we cannot offer to serve as your literary agent. This is not always a reflection of the merit of your submission-- many of the submissions we read are excellent, they just aren't right for us.

We also apologize for the form rejection. The sheer number of queries we receive prevents personalization in order for us to respond in a timely fashion.

We wish you all the best in finding more suitable representation, encourage you to query widely, and thank you for giving us the opportunity to consider your work.

Sincerely,
Shari Maurer
The Stringer Literary Agency LLC

And if you did serve me, I'd tip you 15%, 20% for international and film rights. Oh, well.

Hello, and thank you for the opportunity to review your work. I'm afraid the project isn't a good fit for me, but I wish you all the best in finding representation elsewhere.

All best,
Rachel Beck
Literary Agent
Liza Dawson Associates

Why are they all afraid? The novel is NOT horror. Congrats on your first dad joke, Mila. Maybe I should register a patent for the term "mom joke."

11

Dear Mila,

Thank you for considering The Seymour Agency -- and me -- to represent your work. I truly appreciate the time you took to find and query me. I'm not the right agent to represent this, so I'm passing. I wish you success in finding representation with an agent who will best represent you and your work. Again, thank you for allowing me the opportunity to review your material.

Best,
Marisa Cleveland

Intellectual property law is pretty far afield of my wheelhouse, but if it's mom jokes, wouldn't I need a "matent"?

Thank you for giving me a chance to consider your work.

Unfortunately I don't believe I'm the right person to represent this effectively.

Publishing is a subjective industry by nature so don't be discouraged. I wish you the best of luck finding an agent who can represent your work with the enthusiasm it deserves.

Best,

Adam Schear
DeFiore and Company
47 East 19th Street, 3rd Floor
New York, NY 10003
T. 212.925.7744 x109
F. 212.925.9803
adam@defliterary.com

Oh, c'mon, Adam! You're not the right person; I'm a bad girl — we'd be the perfect literary match. You could have sold my manuscript without enthusiasm. The main word there is "sold."

13

Dear Mila,

Thank you so much for giving me a chance to consider your work. Unfortunately, I don't believe I'm the right person to represent it effectively.

Publishing is such a subjective industry; so, please don't be discouraged. I wish you the absolute best of luck finding an agent who can represent your work with the enthusiasm it deserves.

All best,
Rebecca Strauss

Do all agents just copy paste the same rejection text? Who wrote the template? I hope it's protected under copyright. Considering the number of times this template's used, the author must be super rich.

Fairbank Literary is at the Bologna Book Fair! Back in the office on March 16th. Anything not urgent will be handled shortly thereafter. Thank you!

MMM... I'd kill for a bologna sandwich with mayo and pickles right now.

15

Dear Mila,

Thank you for sending me TEN MYRIAD MOVES. After review of your query and sample pages, I have decided to pass on this project.

Keep in mind that Publishing is a subjective industry and what may not work for me, may be exactly what another agent is looking for. Thank you so much for the opportunity of reviewing your query and I wish you the best of luck in your writing career.

Sincerely,

Kat Kerr
Literary Agent
Donald Maass Literary Agency

Okay, this is not going the way I thought it would. But life goes on, and there's a lot to do and see in New York City.

Dear Author,

Thanks so much for letting us take a look at your materials, and please forgive me for responding with a form letter. The volume of submissions we receive, however, makes it impossible to correspond with everyone personally.

Unfortunately, the project you describe does not suit our list at this time. We wish you the best of luck in finding an agent and publisher for your work, and we thank you, once again, for letting us consider your materials.

Sincerely,
Michael Bourret

Michael W. Bourret
(213) 455-4082
mbourret@dystel.com
@michaelbourret | he/him

The word abbreviation
is way too long.

Thank you for letting us consider this but unfortunately we're not going to take it further. We wish you all the best of luck in finding representation elsewhere.

Best wishes
Northbank Talent Management

Which one is it: fortunately or un-fortunately? Unfortunately... Eh... I went to Central Park today and saw an addict on a bench cooking dope. And they say New Yorkers don't like to cook and always order delivery.

Your query has landed safely in our inbox. As we mentioned on our website, we will read and review your query. If we feel we can help, we will be in touch. If you have not heard from us within two months, you can assume we will not be able to represent your work.

Thank you for your interest in WordServe!

Please check out these helpful books on Amazon:

Excelling at the Craft of Writing - 101 Ideas to Move Your Prose to the Next Level

Overachieving Your Platform - 95 Ideas to Embrace Your Inner Sales Marketing Genius

Today I fixed my toilet flush that was making an annoyingly loud noise. I think one of my ovaries dropped and turned into a ball.

Dear Mila,

I'm sorry I didn't see your query when it first landed and want you to know how seriously we consider each project we receive at Folio. I am sorry to say, though, that unfortunately I do not have a place on my current list to take this on.

Please keep in mind that every agent has different tastes and sensibilities and more or less bandwidth to take on new projects at any given time. And this is a crazily subjective business. What does not work for one agent may work perfectly for another, and I encourage you to continue your search for someone to champion your work, and trust you will find the agent (or publisher) your work absolutely clicks with.

Please know I wish you all the best,

Jeff Silberman

I know you do.
You are forgiven, Jeff.

Dear Mila,

Thank you so much for sending TEN MYRIAD MOVES. It's a wonderful story idea, but unfortunately, I didn't fall in love with this draft as much as I would need to take on the project. For that reason, I am going to step aside for now, but I truly appreciate the opportunity to consider your work.

I wish you the very best of luck with this and all of your projects!

Best,

Jennifer Herrington
Associate Agent
Harvey Klinger Literary Agency
300 W 55th St. 11V
New York, NY 10019

A 3-year-old girl got out of the car window and kept yelling "Why does that matter? Why does that matter?" I don't know, kid! I really don't.

21

Dear Mila,

Thank you for your query. Please know I carefully considered your project, but I don't feel I can offer representation at this time. The marketplace is more selective than ever and I must keep a modest list.

I appreciate the opportunity to consider, however, I don't feel I have a clear editorial vision for this project. Nevertheless, I wish you every success with TEN MYRIAD MOVES! Don't give up!

Keep going with it, there are numerous agents out there that may be a good fit. I wish you the best of luck!

Warmly,
Dorian Maffei

In sci-fi, every character wears one personalized uniform all the time. In reality, a fashion attempt to make leggings the uniform failed. Thank god!

Dear Mila,

Thanks so much for letting me take a look at your materials, and please forgive me for responding with a form letter. The volume of submissions we receive, however, makes it impossible to correspond with everyone personally.

Unfortunately, the project you describe does not suit my list at this time. I wish you the best of luck in finding an agent and publisher for your work, and thank you, once again, for letting me consider your materials.

Sincerely,

Amy Bishop

I saw a lady in a top and shoes but no bottom, just underwear. Perhaps that should be our uniform. It'd solve the loneliness problem; or increase STD transmission. I am not fully ready to create public policy yet.

Dear Mila,

Thank you very much for letting us consider
this but I'm afraid that we're going to pass on
this one. We wish you all the best in finding
representation elsewhere.

Best wishes,
Northbank Talent Management

----

www.northbanktalent.com

If you're an adult, you're bored,
exhausted, or annoyed. It's some-
how the mix of those 3 ingredients.
And you lose the words forever and
never. Because never say never
and nothing lasts forever.

Dear Mila,

Thank you for thinking of me for your submission. I read your material with interest but unfortunately I don't feel as passionately about this project as I would need to in order to take it forward, so I'm afraid we're unable to offer you representation for this one.

Wishing you the best of luck in finding an agent.

Kind regards,
Sian Ellis-Martin
sian@blakefriedmann.co.uk

At a restaurant the sensor water faucet didn't work properly. Water ran on and off fast, then on and off again, like a 40-year-old man's dick: hard and not hard fast, hard and not hard again. Make up your mind already!

2
5

Dear Mila,

I hope you are doing well. I truly appreciate you thinking of me for your book and allowing me to review TEN MYRIAD MOVES.

Unfortunately, the story didn't captivate me as I would have liked. I'm sorry to say, I am going to pass on this.

Please know the publishing industry is very subjective and another agent might feel differently. That said, don't give up and keep working on your craft. I wish you the very best of luck in your writing endeavors.

Best,

Mariah Nichols
D4EO Literary Agency

Unfortunately...will pass...yeah.
Now what should I get for lunch?
Korean or Indian?

21

Dear Mila,

Thank you so much for giving me a chance to consider TEN MYRIAD MOVES. Unfortunately this doesn't feel like the right project for me at this time. I'm so sorry, but this is a pass for me.

Please remember that this is a highly subjective industry, and what doesn't work for me may be exactly what another agent loves. It only takes one yes to get you in the door!

I wish you the best of luck in your search! And I hope you'll keep me in mind should you be seeking representation for another project in the future.

With gratitude,
Colleen Oefelein
Literary Agent
Working alongside Macgregor & Luedeke Literary
Adventure Write Literary Management
The Mayflower Building
4901 E Mayflower Ln
Wasilla, Alaska 99654
colleen@adventurewrite.com
www.AdventureWrite.com
Facebook: Colleen Oefelein
Celebrating 13 years in the arts!

I remember. I remember everything.

21

Dear Mila,

Thanks so much for your query.

I'm afraid your book just doesn't sound like a good fit for my list at this time.

I wish you all the best with your career and hope you find the right agent match soon.

Best,
Kim Lionetti

You all claim you can and want to help with a writer's career — to kickstart, boost, and level it up. And then you pass, but send all the best wishes. Also, you prefer a writer with an established name, online presence, and sales, so already with a career. If I had all that, why would I need an agent?

Dear Mila,

Thank you for sending me your submission for
TEN MYRIAD MOVES. I appreciate your patience as
I reviewed your work. While it really has a lot
of merit, I'm sorry to say that the material
does not seem to be a fit for my list at this
time, and so I must pass.

Thank you for the opportunity, and all best
wishes,
    Michelle Grajkowski

There're 3 types of pregnant
people representing birth emojis
in iMessage: a woman with
long hair, a woman with short
hair, and a man with short hair.
Hahaha!

Dear Mila,

Thank you for giving me the opportunity to consider representing TEN MYRIAD MOVES. I apologize for taking so long to reply.

I've decided to pass on this.

After a great amount of consideration, I've made the difficult decision to considerably reduce the amount of new work that I take on at this time. My client list has grown and become very full, which consumes most of my work time.

I encourage you to send your work to other agents, so that it can receive adequate attention.

I appreciate your interest in my agency. I wish you the very best with your writing and success in publishing your work.

Sincerely,
Pam

--

Pamela Hopkins
Literary Agent
Hopkins Literary Associates
hlasubmissions@gmail.com

What happens to cut foreskin?
Is it recycled?

30

Dear Mila,
I'm sorry, but I'm just not the right agent
for your project and so I will have to pass.
Thank you for considering me and best of luck
with your future queries.

Sincerely,

Lori Galvin

Whenever someone calls me
Ma'am, I instantly feel like
I'm standing in a long line at
a local DMV on a hot summer
afternoon, their online system
is down, the AC barely works,
and I silently cuss in every
language I know.

Dear Mila,
I'm sorry, but your project does not sound like a fit for me at this time, and so I will have to pass. Thank you for considering me and best of luck with your future queries.

Sincerely,

Laura Bradford

--
Laura Bradford (she/her)
Literary Agent
Bradford Literary Agency
619/521-1201 Office
619/929-1633 Cell
www.bradfordlit.com

I heard about a tech company that converts CO2 into bricks. Amazing. 10 people fart and ta-da! A townhouse.

Thank you for your email. I am currently closed to queries. I will re-open on Tuesday, September 7, and will be using Query Manager at that point. You can submit at this link: https://QueryManager.com/BridgetSmith

Best of luck with your writing!

Sincerely,
Bridget Smith

One word that automatically makes people feel weird, empathetic, offended, supportive, scared, opinionated, tolerant, and indifferent. Tra-aa-ans-gender!

We have received your query.   If you have followed our submission guidelines we will review your work. Due to the large number of queries we receive, we can only respond to those we are interested in--if you have not received a response within 90 days of submitting it is safe to assume that we have passed on your work.

Please note that Jennifer Schober is no longer with our agency. Karen Solem and Amanda Leuck are no longer accepting unsolicited submissions.

Also note that Ali Herring only accepts submissions through Query Manager, not through this email.

Thank you for submitting to Spencerhill Associates.

"Mila, I've always heard the life of a writer is lonely. Can you confirm or deny this?" someone asked me.
"Propaganda of which country spreads this information?"

vskurnick@lgrliterary.com
Re: Query

Thanks but not for me.

Craigslist ad: Gently used dildos.
"I have too many dildos and wouldn't
mind giving a couple away. Some are
nice and big. I always clean them
really well before and after each
use. It's a waste to throw them out,
so I thought I'd see if anyone would
want them. This ad is for mature
discreet men only. Please be serious.
I'm not looking to embarrass anyone
or myself. I'm in Maspeth, Queens
and can meet in or near the Grover
Cleveland park area." It's good to
know there are still nice and gener-
ous people out there.

submissions@deniseshannonagency.com
Re: Query

Thank you for your recent query to the Denise
Shannon Literary Agency. Unfortunately, we do
not feel your project is right for us, but we
wish you the best of luck elsewhere.

Rejection AND they killed James Bond?
2 misfortunes in 1 day.

6

Thank you for your email!

I am currently closed to queries, and will reopen at a later date. Please check the Gelf-man Schneider website or my Twitter account (@penelopekayb) for updates.

If you have a query or solicited material with me, I look forward to responding to you soon! Please let me know if there are any updates on your end, particularly if you've received an offer of representation!

Please also note that while I do read & respond to each query, the volume of queries I receive sometimes makes a personal reply impossible and I may use a form response for the sake of expediency.

Thank you!

Penelope Burns

According to the advertisement, I'm supposed to use a menstrual cup, for the environment and blah blah? Sure. I'll have a cup of rosé.

Thank you for thinking of me in connection with your writing. I'm not the right match for you on this, but I wish you all good luck placing it in the right hands.

Marianne Merola
Brandt & Hochman Literary Agents, Inc.
The Joy Harris Literary Agency, Inc.
1501 Broadway, #2605, New York, NY 10036
Ph: 212-840-5773 | Fax: 212-840-5776
mmerola@bromasite.com
www.brandthochman.com
www.joyharrisagency.com
Sent from my iPhone

Oh, an automated text message from my physician: "Review the Vitamin D prescription Doctor wrote you. Reply stop to opt-out."
What can I say, doc? Vitamin D is great. 5 stars! And the prescription is so awesome that it should have its own Netflix show.

Dear Mila,

Thanks for sharing your query letter with me. I regret to inform you that I won't be requesting additional materials or offering representation.

Please know I can only responsibly take on a few new clients each year, and my decision to pass does not mean another agent won't be a passionate and energetic advocate for your project.

Please accept my very best wishes for your writing success.

Respectfully,

Adriann

ADRIANN RANTA ZURHELLEN
LITERARY AGENT
Folio Literary Management | Folio Jr.
630 9th Avenue, Suite 1101,
New York, NY 10036
FolioLit.com

Do embassies pay rent for their buildings?

39

Hi,

Thank you so much! I just want to confirm that I received your query.

It might be up to 60 days on this! I'm sorry to make you wait, I know it's torment. If you do not hear from me after 60 days, please consider this a pass on your submission. Please do contact me if I am considering your work and you have received an offer from another agent or an editor.

Best,
Dani
--

Dani Segelbaum | Literary Agent
Carol Mann Agency
55 Fifth Avenue, New York, NY 10003
http://www.carolmannagency.com/

Boyfriend jeans, girlfriend jeans, mom jeans. There are more types of jeans than family members.

Dear Author:

Thanks so much for letting us take a look at your materials and please forgive us for responding with a form letter. The volume of submissions we receive, however, makes it impossible to correspond with everyone personally.

Unfortunately, the project you describe does not suit our list at this time. We wish you the best of luck in finding an agent and publisher for your work and we thank you, once again, for letting us consider your materials.

Sincerely,
Jim McCarthy

Jim McCarthy
Vice President
Dystel, Goderich & Bourret
212-627-9100 x707

The beauty industry is not for you to look better — it's for you to stay looking the same.

41

Dear Author,

Thanks so much for letting us take a look at your materials, and please forgive me for responding with a form letter. The volume of submissions we receive, however, makes it impossible to correspond with everyone personally.

Unfortunately, the project you describe does not suit our list at this time. We wish you the best of luck in finding an agent and publisher for your work, and we thank you, once again, for letting us consider your materials.

Sincerely,
Dystel, Goderich & Bourret LLC

*****Requested material should be sent to this email address unless otherwise specified, but please note that this email is not monitored at all times for other types of correspondence. Please address any questions regarding our responses to your material to the email address of the appropriate agent by consulting the staff page of our website at http:// www.dystel.com .*****

Has anyone ever seen THE LIST?

Thanks, Mila. Good for you! I'm afraid that
this isn't quite right for my list, but I wish
you the best.

Joelle Delbourgo

--

Joëlle Delbourgo (she/hers)
Joëlle Delbourgo Associates
101 Park St.
Montclair, NJ 07042
joelle@delbourgo.com
973-773-0836
www.delbourgo.com
Follow me on Twitter: @jldelbourgo & *Facebook:* https://www.facebook.com/joelledelbour-
goassoc

No, I don't want to follow
you on socials. I don't care
what you eat, where you
travel to, how big your ass
is, or how many manuscripts
you have sold to publishers.

Thank you for giving G Agency the chance to consider your work. Unfortunately, we are only taking on a short list of new clients at this time, and have decided that your project isn't the right fit for us.

Reading tastes are subjective, and another agent might feel more enthusiasm for your work. Do keep up the hard work of submitting, as you never know where you'll make the connection that makes your book happen.

Best,
G Agency Submissions

G... The book happened when it was written.

Dear Ms. Mila,

Thank you so much for your query. Unfortunately, however, this project doesn't sound
right for me. I encourage you to continue to
submit elsewhere, and I wish you every success
in your writing career. Thanks again for thinking of me.

Cordially,
Diana Fox

Once, someone asked me: "What is your
work process like as a writer?" Well,
first thing in the morning, I need a cup
of coffee, the beans of which were
grown by a virgin; and a massage
by twins Capuchins. Yes, the monkeys
must be brothers, or else I won't get
inspiration for the day. Then I need
the sun shining onto my work desk at
exactly 45 degrees... What do you
mean work process?! You sit down and
write!

Thank you so much for your email. If you've sent us a query, we promise we'll be reviewing each submission, but please understand that due to the volume of emails we receive, it is now our policy to respond only if we are interested in seeing more material. Furthermore, Rebecca Gardner and Courtney Gatewood are closed to queries.

If you are reaching out with an author request, rights inquiry, or other business matter, we will try to be in touch as soon as possible.

Thanks again for thinking of us. We sincerely wish you all the best.

Warm regards,
The Gernert Company

If you're writing about submission — press 1. If you want to buy us dinner — press 2. For the DNA test — press 3. To hear the word "the list" 14 times in a row — stay on the line, and someone will be with you shortly.

Hi Mila,

Thanks for this. We're a small agency, and very selective, especially on fiction, and your synopsis didn't seem quite right for us. Another agent will surely see it differently. Best of luck with it.

Kind regards

Paul Feldstein
The Feldstein Agency
54 Abbey Street
Bangor BT20 4JB
N. Ireland U.K.
Phone: 44(0)2891312485 (NOTE: New Number)
paul@thefeldsteinagency.co.uk
www.thefeldsteinagency.co.uk

The content of this email is confidential and intended only for the recipient(s) specified. It is strictly forbidden to share any part of this message with any third party, without the written consent of the sender. If you received this message by mistake, please advise by replying to this message and delete it.

You use Google hosting for email.
None of your content is confidential.

Thank you for submitting your query to me here at KT Literary.

Please know that I read all queries myself and consider each and every submission carefully. Unfortunately, I am going to pass on asking to read the full manuscript of this book - I'm sorry. I wish you the very best in your agent hunt!

Sincerely,
Sara Megibow
she/her
KT Literary, LLC
twitter @SaraMegibow
Always LGBTQIA+ Friendly!
https://www.publishersmarketplace.com/members/SaraMegibow/

In my hunt for an agent I don't kill it — I let it free in the wild.

You are receiving this email because I am no longer accepting submissions via email. As of **March 19, 2019,** I am only accepting submissions via the Query Manager form above my bio on our website.

I am excited and eager to read your work. However, I ask that you please use my new Query Manager Form, follow the directions on how to submit your work to me at this link:

https://querymanager.com/query/JenniferMarch-Soloway

Query manager helps me manage my submissions and respond faster as a result. I appreciate you taking the extra step to help me read and reply to you faster than via email.

Thank you for thinking of me, and please consider sending me a query via the form. I love a good story and hope to read yours!

Best,
Jennifer

There's no follow up option in Query-Manager. It's very impersonal. I'd rather talk to Siri — at least it responds, with nonsense, but it responds.

Dear Mila,

Thank you so much for thinking of me.

I find the premise and setting of TEN MYRIAD MOVES intriguing, and there is much to recommend about the story. However, I wouldn't be the right agent for this project. For this reason, I am passing and stepping aside.

Mila, I am so sorry not to offer you representation at this time. I have no doubt you will have great success with TEN MYRIAD MOVES, and I wish you the very best of publishing luck as you move forward.

Thank you again for thinking of me. I truly appreciate the opportunity to consider your work.

Best,
Jennifer

Jennifer, oh dear Jennifer. I wasn't thinking of you. You were on the list of agents, just like other 200 agents who represent fiction. Thank you for making it seem personal. It's not.

Hi Mila,

Thank you for letting me know, and thank you for your original query. It sounds like a fun caper of a story, and your work I was able to view on your website is lively and interesting, but I don't think this is the right fit for me at this time. Congratulations on your offer and best of luck as you move forward with your work.

All the best,
Alice

Alice Fugate
The Joy Harris Literary Agency, inc.
1501 Broadway Suite 2605
New York, New York 10036
Ph: 212 924-6269
Fax: 212 840-5776
alice@joyharrisliterary.com
www.joyharrisliterary.com

My eye doctor knows how to say
"I'm tired" in 50 languages.
I should learn too.

Wishing you the best - your book sounds wonderful but I'm cutting back now and not taking
on many new fiction clients.

Ellen Geiger
Frances Goldin Literary Agency, Inc.

So yeah, I got an offer of representation and got signed up
by an agent. After half a year
of him querying publishers I
started to come up with selling
strategy ideas and shared
those with him. I pushed him to
change the approach. He said he
was on it once the weather got
warmer so he could leave the house.
I knew I had made a mistake...
and continued querying agents.

feliciaeth.literary@gmail.com
Re: Query

Thanks but this doesn't seem line the right
match for my small list.

Sent from my iPhone

No troblem at old.

Hi Mila,

Thanks for reaching out, but the premise doesn't sound right for me.

All my best,
Victoria Marini

If you receive an offer of representation, Congrats! Please, do let me know so I can respond to your query or to any requested material in a more urgent fashion
Please note, this email is for queries only! If (and only if) you are inquiring about sub-rights, media, publicity, marketing or another matter related to one of my clients or titles, please e-mail me directly at Victoria@irenegoodman.com. Please, *please,* Don't send queries directly to this address, as they'll be deleted!
Thank you!

Double please? Poor Victoria. I feel you. Some people are dumb in following instructions. Worse is when you use 7 exclamation points to be heard. If you have to yell to be heard, you're doing something WRONG.

Dear Mila,

After much consideration, I'll be regretfully stepping aside instead of throwing my hat into the ring.

Wishing you the very best of luck in your publishing endeavors.

Sincerely,
Lucy Carson

Lucy Carson, Lucy Carson...Where have I heard this name before? Was there a famous actress with that name or something? The first and last name combination is so simple and memorable that it sounds almost made up. Perfect for a TV commercial or a thief.

Congrats! We do not reply fiction so best of luck.

Janis A. Donnaud
917 402-2663 cell phone

At different times, I went on a date with a doctor, an FBI agent, a Marine, a police officer, and a fireman — the royal flesh in first responders poker.

adriann@foliolit.com
Re: Automatic reply: QUERY "Ten Myriad Moves"

Hello! I am away from my desk until Mon, Jan. 3rd. If this is an emergency, you can reach me at 917-971-3352, otherwise I look forward to being in touch when I return.

Wishing you a peaceful, restorative holiday season!

Thanks,

Adriann

Why do people on Park Avenue use so much perfume?

Thanks for writing but I'm not taking on new projects.

Best of luck!
JEFF KLEINMAN

FOUNDING PARTNER | LITERARY AGENT

Folio Literary Management | Folio Jr.
630 9th Avenue, Suite 1101,
New York, NY 10036
212-400-1494 x 240 (O) | 212-727-7001 ©
jeff@foliolit.com | FolioLit.com

I forgot I had queried him before. Bcc can do that to you.

58

Dear Milla,

Thanks for your query.
Unfortunately, I'm afraid I'm not the right agent for this project. I wish you much luck in getting it published.

All best,
Caryn

Caryn Karmatz Rudy (she/her)
DeFiore and Company Literary Management Inc.
47 East 19th Street, 3rd Floor
New York, NY 10003
T. 212 925 7744 Ext. 115
F. 212 925 9803
caryn@defliterary.com

All people should hang a map of the world in their toilets. This way, unavoidably, they'll learn geography, finally.

Thank you for your email.

If your request is administrative, it will be answered promptly.

If you have submitted a query, we appreciate your patience. As we receive many submissions, we cannot send personal rejections letters; if you have not heard from us in 4 to 6 weeks, unfortunately we will not be pursuing your project.

Please note that we do not accept email attachments, and your submission will not be read if there is an attachment.

Sincerely,
DCLA

What if my new novel sucks this much that no one wants to represent it? Nah, this can't be it. Princeton and Columbia Universities added one of my fiction books to their libraries. And that itself means something.

You are receiving this message as confirmation that your query was received.

If you are inquiring about literary representation and <u>have not done so already</u>, please email your query letter with the first 50 pages of your manuscript or proposal attached as a **docx.** file. If you need to follow up your query with your manuscript attachment, please include it as a reply in your **original email thread**. <u>Do not reply to this email.</u>

For detailed query guidelines and information about our agents and clients, visit our website: www.jillgrinbergliterary.com

While we endeavor to respond to every query, due to the volume of submissions we receive and our commitments to our existing client list, it may not always be possible. If we decide to pursue your submission, we will be in touch with you. We appreciate your understanding, and we look forward to reading your work.

Jill Grinberg Literary Management
392 Vanderbilt Avenue
Brooklyn, NY 11238 |
www.jillgrinbergliterary.com

Please do not respond to this email unless requested.

Send a query, but don't email us under any circumstances. Sit down and come here. Stop talking and tell the truth.

Thank you for considering Victoria Sanders & Associates as a potential agency to represent your work. We have reviewed the material you sent and we regret that we will not be offering to review your work further at this time. Please know that we are very selective with the materials that we request. We encourage you to keep writing and we wish you every success. Please forgive this impersonal note. We receive a tremendous number of queries and are forced to focus our attention on a limited number of projects.

Kind regards,
Victoria Sanders

Why do agents encourage me to continue writing? Your rejection won't make me stop writing LOL. It's a very subjective industry, remember?

Thank you for sending your submission to The Book Group. We appreciate the work that goes into querying and we're glad you sought us out. We receive so many queries that we aren't able to respond individually to each one. The agent to whom you sent your query will be in touch as soon as possible if she would like to pursue your work. If you don't hear from an agent within three months, it means we're declining the opportunity to represent you. Some housekeeping: Please make sure that you've included the first and last name of the agent you are querying in the subject line of your email.

You are welcome to submit to more than one agent at once at The Book Group; please let us know that you've submitted to multiple agents on our team in the body of your query letter.

We understand that you may have sent your query to other agencies. If you receive an offer of representation from another agency, we'd be grateful if you could let us know by sending another email with "offer of representation" in the subject line.

For our complete submissions guidelines and to get a better idea of the best agent for your book, please visit our website at www.thebookgroup.com. For inquiries that are not related to representation, please email info@thebookgroup.com. Thank you again for sharing your work with us.

With all best wishes,
The Book Group

So many useless words...

Not for me, thanks.

_____

Cordially,

WordWise Submissions

And the best rejection letter,
according to Mila's Awards,
goes to (intrigue, intrigue)
WordWise! Congratulations!

Thank you for your query. We respect the time and effort that creators put into the querying process, and this is a courtesy auto-response to acknowledge receipt of your submission. If you do not receive a request from us for a further materials **within three months from submission**, please consider it a pass. If we make a request, the requesting agent will advise you of their reading timeline once the full manuscript or other requested materials have been received. If you receive an offer of representation during the three-month consideration window or while a Root Literary agent is considering your full manuscript/materials, please send an alert before accepting an offer of representation. Thank you, and we look forward to considering your work!

Taylor Haggerty (she|her)
rootliterary.com
3727 W. Magnolia Blvd #205, Burbank, CA 91505

Would it take your intern 3 months to read an alert too?

Mila Ilkova (bitch | that bitch)
New York, NY

65

Thank you for querying.

Your query has been received and will be reviewed by our team. If you don't hear from us within eight weeks, it means that we will be passing on your work.

Please don't take a pass as a comment on you or your writing ability; it isn't intended to be one.

We wish you the best of luck with your submissions.

Sincerely,
The New Leaf Literary Team

*Please do not respond as this is an automated response.

--
New Leaf Literary & Media
110 W 40th St, Suite 2201
New York, NY 10018
www.newleafliterary.com

I really miss the optimism of the 1990s. Those were great times.

Dear Mila,

Thank you very much for submitting your material "Ten Myriad Moves" to us.

Our agents have now had a chance to look at it and we are sorry to say we don't feel that we can offer you representation. Because of the high volume of submissions we receive, unfortunately we are not able to give you more detailed feedback than this. However, these things are very subjective and someone else may well feel differently about your work.

Thank you again for letting us take a look at your material, and we wish you the best of luck in finding an agent and publisher.

Best wishes,
Submissions AM Heath & Co Ltd

Why do agencies assume that their OPINION is an ultimate one? I know that others may feel differently about my work.

Thank you for your email. I am away from my desk, returning January 5.

Querying writers: I will respond to your query by January 12 only if I wish to read more. If you have not received a response by January 12, it is a pass.

Thank you for your patience and understanding. May you have a safe, peaceful holiday season and a joyful 2022!

Best,
Laura
laura@triadaus.com

This is a convenient type of professional ghosting, with the specific deadline and all. Knowing what's going on is important. Good job! Thank you!

Hello and thank you for thinking of The Seymour Agency!

Your submission is important to us. Please know that every query is given extensive consideration. If we do not respond with a request for additional material within three weeks, we have elected to pass. This means that the material is not right for us at this time, but this is subjective, and another agent or editor may feel differently. Do NOT be discouraged. As with any partnership, it is important to find the best match.

If we have requested a full or partial of your manuscript, please follow up for a response after nine weeks. Bear in mind that oftentimes a project may receive multiple reads before a decision is reached.

In all of your endeavors, we wish you the best, and we thank you for the privilege to review your work.

Many thanks,
Jennifer

I hate long rejection letters full of bullshit words that mean nothing.

Submit@ZimmAgency.com
[Auto-Reply] Query "Ten Myriad Moves"

Thank you so much for your submission. This auto-reply is intended as a verification that your email has been received. If the agency is interested in your material, we will be in touch within two weeks. Meanwhile, I curate a blog that talks about publishing industry news and advice for writers. If you're interested, please click the following link and you will be directed to the page. www.Project-Publish.com/blog

Best,
Helen

Another latent writer who has all the time in the world to write a blog but not an email.

To Mila

Thank you for submitting to Prospect Agency! We look forward to reading the uploaded sample manuscript, Ten Myriad Moves. We appreciate your patience while we review your work. In most cases, you should expect to hear a re- sponse within three months. Please keep this receipt for your records.

Respectfully,
Prospect Agency

Submission Id:5680532021131211306835

Prospect Agency LLC
551 Valley Rd., PMB 377
Upper Montclair, NJ 07043
www.prospectagency.com

Rejection receipt for my records? I want to be able to deduct stupidity on my next tax return because I spent so much on it, way more than on office supplies.

Thank you for your query. This is an auto-reply to acknowledge receipt of your message. Due to the high number of queries I receive every day, I am unfortunately unable to respond to each. If I am interested in reading more of your work, I will send you a request for material. If you do not receive a request from me within 4 weeks, it means I don't believe I'm the right agent for your project, and no further response will be sent. Please note that I do not represent screenplays.

Thank you and best wishes,
Lisa Erbach Vance

Attention! Attention!
The book agent is missing.
She's very polite and patient,
reads a lot, doesn't like attachments, and knows a few tricks,
like how to waste 3 months. Her
name's Unfortunately. Last seen
in Europe. Anyone who finds her
gets a reward: 15%. Fuck it, 20%

   Thank you for your query. We appreciate the
opportunity to review your submission. Due to
the volume of submissions we receive, we will
respond only if we are interested in requesting
more material. If you have not received a request from us within 12 weeks, consider that we
have passed.

   Thank you,

   The Stonesong team

My hair needs more volume.
Thanks for the reminder to
buy a styling product.

Dear author,

Thank you for submitting your work to Susanna Lea Associates, we look forward to reading. Due to the volume of submissions we receive and our limited staff, we can respond only to queries we are interested in and cannot guarantee a response or editorial advice to those we decline. We do read everything, typically within 6-12 weeks.

Please do not call the office in request of an update.

For news about our agency, we encourage you to follow us on social media.

Twitter | Instagram | Facebook

Thank you and all the best,
Susanna Lea Associates
--
Susanna Lea Associates
331 W. 20th St.
New York, NY 10011
www.susannalea.com

Do not call us, do not contact us in any way, and forget we even exist.

14

Merci pour votre envoi. Malheureusement, en raison de l'importante quantité de textes que nous recevons, nous ne vous recontacterons qu'en cas de réponse positive. Nous ne donnons pas de conseils éditoriaux sur les manuscrits que nous refusons. Le temps d'étude d'un manuscrit est généralement de 6 à 12 semaines.

Cordialement,
Susanna Lea Associates

They started rejecting me in French. Enchanté.

15

Thank you for the interest you've expressed in Books & Such representing your work. We understand that your query is a statement of trust in us to treat your creative work with care and respect. In turn, we assure you that every query we receive is read and evaluated. However, the number of queries we receive has grown considerably, causing us to spend a large percentage of our days responding to queries. As we considered how to remain responsive to submissions while being good managers of our time, we concluded that we will only contact those writers from whom we want to see more material. If you don't hear from us asking to see more of your writing within 30 days after you have sent your email, please know that we have read and considered your submission but determined that it would not be a good fit for us.

We appreciate the work you put into your creative efforts, which is why we handle your submission with care.

If you are submitting to Rachelle Gardner, she is no longer an agent with Books & Such.

--

The Books & Such Staff

> My query is a statement of work that must be converted into a $200k bank deposit very soon.

11

Aevitas no-reply@aevitascreative.com
Re: Your submission to Jon Michael Darga

Thank you for your query. Unfortunately, in light of the high volume of submissions we receive, we cannot reply to every submission.

Anytime I see in the street a truck or a minivan with a sign on it like "Three Plumbing Guys" or "Hammertime Interior Inc." or "Quality Building Supplies," I automatically assume it's FBI working undercover.

11

Thank you for your interest in the agency.
We are closed to queries through March 2022.
Queries received in the meantime will be deleted. If you sent an email to this account regarding permission to quote from the work of
one of our authors, if your request is in re-
gard to foreign or film rights to the work our
authors, or if your query is a direct referral
from one of our authors, please email
sarah@francescollin.com We look forward to re-
opening to new clients in 2022.

Who comes up with ideas and public policies? Take porn for instance. Who decides that this is the way we are supposed to fuck? Ministry of porn?

Dear Writer:

Thank you for your inquiry. We are sorry that
we cannot invite you to submit your work or offer to represent you. Moreover, we apologize
that we cannot respond in a more personal manner.

We wish you the best of luck elsewhere.

Sincerely,

Dunham Literary, Inc.

A pack of salt is endless.
You buy it for life. You
change apartments, even
cities, and you move the
pack of salt with you. When
it's finally over — it feels
like the end of an era.

19

Thanks, Mila. Good for you! I'm afraid that this isn't quite right for my list, but I wish you the best.

Joelle Delbourgo

You suffer from instability, but as soon as you get settled, you are surely drawn to adventures, to traveling from one place to another to get, yet again, that fresh feeling of the unknown, the unpredictable — the instability.

Hello,

I am no longer working as an Agent. If this is an urgent matter, please reach out to Lesley Sabga, lesley@theseymouragency.com, or Nicole Resciniti, nicole@theseymouragency.com.

All best,
Kat

I keep singing a tune and I'm not sure whether I heard it somewhere or I totally created it myself. Guess I'll never know.

Hello! Thank you for thinking of The Seymour Agency.

Your submission is important to us. Please know that every query is given extensive consideration. If we do not respond with a request for additional materials within three weeks, then we have elected to pass. This means the project was not right for us at this time. This is entirely subjective! Do NOT be discouraged. Another agent or editor may feel differently.

If we have requested a full or partial of your manuscript, please follow up for a response after nine weeks. Bear in mind that a manuscript may receive multiple reads before a decision is reached. In all of your endeavors, we wish you the very best, and we are very thankful for the opportunity and privilege to review your work.

Best,

Nicole Resciniti
The Seymour Agency

Fun plan for the night: buy wine and annoy ex with drunken texts of past unresolved issues. Woohoo!

Thank you so much for your submission! Our submission guidelines have changed and we are no longer accepting email submissions to this inbox. Please visit our website, www.three-seasagency.com/submissions for further instructions. We look forward to reading your work!

All best wishes,
Michelle, Cori and Stacey

There should be a version of the FDA for agents: a unified way to offer them 15% of your future money. Because their guidelines clearly aren't working: query letter only, query letter and 3 pages, first chapter, first 3 chapters, NO ATTACHMENTS AT ALL!!!, query and synopsis, elevator's pitch and pitch deck, this font and that font, double space and word doc, pdf only and specific subject line. Who are you kidding? No one reads anything anyway anymore.

Dear Author:

Thank you. We have received your query.

Because of the high volume of email submissions we receive, we will only get in touch with you if we are interested in your project; if we are interested in your work, we will be in touch within six to eight weeks.

Thank you.

The Irene Goodman Literary Agency

This rejection letter is wordy, repetitive, and needs editing.

Dear Mila,

Thank you so much for submitting sample pages of TEN MYRIAD MOVES to me. Even though I found many great qualities in your work, I wasn't drawn in as deeply as I hoped to be, so I must decline it at this time.

I'm sorry to not have better news to share. The publishing industry is very subjective, so what may not work for me could be just what another agent is looking for. I encourage you to continue your pursuit of publication. I wish you the very best of luck!

Sincerely,
Amy

Amy Giuffrida
Associate Agent
The Jennifer De Chiara Literary Agency
New York - Los Angeles - Chicago
amy.jdlit@gmail.com
www.jdlit.com
Twitter: @kissedbyink
Instagram: kissedbyink

I waNNa play dRums.

Dear Mila,

Thank you for thinking of me for TEN MYRIAD
MOVES. I enjoyed reading your query and sample
pages, but I'm sorry to say this project isn't
for me. I'm extremely selective about the adult
work I take on, focusing much more heavily on
children's lit, and this didn't quite land in
the sweet spot for me.

Please be assured querying is a subjective
business. I wish you all the best in finding
the right agent.

Sincerely,
--
Savannah Brooks
Associate Literary Agent
The Jennifer De Chiara Literary Agency
www.jdlit.com
@sblitagent
Celebrating 21 years of making dreams come
true!

Then why mention that you represent
contemporary fiction? There's no
sweet spot between princesses and
a political revolution with dark humor.

I have left The Lotts Agency, and will no
longer be using this email. Should you need assistance, please contact Chris Lotts at
chris@lottsagency.com.

All best,
Lara Lea Allen

--
Lara Lea Allen
The Lotts Agency
68 Jay Street, Suite 201
Brooklyn, NY 11201
lara@lottsagency.com
www.lottsagency.com
tel. 718-414-6870

Phew, good! Fewer people to bcc.

Hello,

Thank you for sending in your query. Due to the high volume of emails we're receiving, it is not possible for us to provide a response to every email. If you don't hear from us within two months, it unfortunately means that your query is not the right fit for our list. If we have requested your manuscript, we will provide a response, though there may be a delay in doing so.

Thank you,
The Lotts Agency

I played drums! It was absolutely awesome! I loved it. My neighbors won't mind if I buy a full drum set and practice at home, right?

Thank you for your submission to The Zoë Pagnamenta Agency. Due to the volume of submissions, we regret that we cannot respond to every query we receive. If we are interested in reading more, we will be in touch with you.

Does Guinness World Records pay for the most rejected writer title? $1M for the lucky loser. Where do I apply?

I am currently closed to new queries. This message will be deleted unread.

This post can tell you why:

https://katemckean.substack.com/p/why-agents-close-to-queries

Best,
Kate McKean
Vice-President & Literary Agent
Howard Morhaim Literary Agency, Inc.
30 Pierrepont St., Brooklyn, NY 11201
kmckean@morhaimliterary.com,
morhaimliterary.com
@kate_mckean

Tinder became more like Instagram: people show off their amazing lives full of vacations and hangouts with friends and exciting adventures, and are not willing to share all that with anyone. No one is good enough for them because "It's Tinder." Shrug-shrug, blink-blink, close-up six-pack.

Dear Mila,

Thank you for thinking of Simon for your query: TEN MYRIAD MOVES.

Unfortunately, your manuscript does not seem like one we could successfully represent at this time. I sincerely offer best wishes and hope you are able to secure properly enthusiastic representation.

All the best,
Dina

Dina A. Williams
Assistant to Simon Lipskar
New Address: 120 Broadway, 22nd floor
New York, NY 10271

Everything looks better with a tan, they say. I sprayed a bit of it on the computer screen — the rejection letter did not get any better.

Dear Mila,

Thank you for your query. Dan Lazar asked me to reply after he evaluated your submission.

We're afraid your project does not seem right for our list, but thank you for thinking of Dan, and best of luck in your search for representation.

Sincerely,

Torie Doherty Munro
Assistant to Dan Lazar

Victoria Doherty Munro
Assistant to Dan Lazar
Writers House LLC
120 Broadway, 22nd Floor
New York, NY 10271

e: vdoherty@writershouse.com
t: 212-685-2400

Life's getting more expensive, money's getting cheaper — I gotta do something. Why don't I have a dead rich distant relative with no family but me?

Hi Mila,

Thank you for the chance to consider your query. Unfortunately, it's not the right fit.

Good luck! And I hope you are healthy and safe.

Tamar
querytamar@contextlit.com

What if I fake to be my agent? I can already fake a smile and an orgasm, so faking something else should not be a problem.

Dear Mila,

Thank you for submitting your query package. After reviewing your materials, I've decided to pass on your project. I can't give more feedback due to the nature of the process.

Best of luck in querying!

Best regards,
Renae Moore
Azantian Literary Agency
www.azantianlitagency.com

I didn't ask for feedback, did I?

Hello,

Thank you for considering WSA for representation. We have received your query and will
reach out if we are interested in pursuing your
project.

Best regards,

Wendy Sherman Associates

--
Wendy Sherman Associates
138 W. 25th St. Suite 1018
New York, NY 10001
Phone: 212-279-9027

Craigslist is still the best:
"Two toys for young kids
that are way too nice to
throw out (the toys)."

submissions@wernickpratt.com
Automatic reply: Query "Ten Myriad Moves"

Thank you for submitting to Wernick & Pratt
Agency. We regret that we cannot respond personally to every submission. If you have not
heard from us within six weeks, please consider
it a pass from the agency.

I want to do something new
for New Year's Eve, like get
a husband. According to the
divorce statistics, marriage
is like buying something on
Amazon with 3,5 stars out of
5. Technically people don't like
it, but some do, so you try it
too because you're willing to
take the risk.

Hello,

I will do my best to read and respond to you within seven weeks of receiving your submission. Unfortunately, due to the volume of submissions received, I am unable to respond to every one personally, so if you haven't heard from me at all by then, it means that I am unable to offer you representation.

Thank you for taking time to send your submissions. I wish you the best of luck through the publication process.

lgsubmissions@defliterary.com

The United States is known for big shots, flu shots, tequila shots, and gunshots. And the American dream is still being given a shot.

Hello,

Thank you for sending us your query. Due to the large volume of submissions we receive, we are unable to respond to each query individually. If an agent is interested in reading more of your work we will be in touch.

Best wishes,

Fletcher & Company

Kindness is a luxury; empathy, a genuine smile from a stranger, and having emergency contact are all a luxury. Love is the ultimate luxury, and not shiny blazers, couches, and trendy fuchsia color this season.

This is an automated reply to acknowledge receipt of your query.

Thank you for submitting your work to Betsy
Amster Literary Enterprises. Please understand
that owing to the volume of queries we receive,
we can only respond further to those that interest us.

There is NO aNgRy way
to say bubbles.

Dear Ms. Mila

No thank you, but thank you for writing to me about TEN MYRIAD MOVES.

Yours sincerely,

William Reiss

John Hawkins & Associates, Inc.

Eat, pray, love.
Save, endure, wait.

Thank you for sending your query. This reply is to let you know that we received it and will give it careful consideration.

Due to the volume of submissions we will only respond again to those projects we wish to pursue.

All best,
BJ Robbins Literary Agency

I played the famous Cinderella game aka cleaning, laundry, cooking. And I talked to a bird, almost like in a fairy tale, except that motherfucker was screaming nonstop. Then another pigeon joined and they started having sex on my fire escape. Now, where's my prince with a foot fetish?

101

We have received your query. If you have followed our submission guidelines we will review
your work. Due to the large number of queries
we receive, we can only respond to those we are
interested in--if you have not received a response within 90 days of submitting it is safe
to assume that we have passed on your work.

Please note that Jennifer Schober is no
longer with our agency. Karen Solem and Amanda
Leuck are no longer accepting unsolicited submissions.

Also note that Ali Herring only accepts submissions through Query Manager, not through
this email.

Thank you for submitting to Spencerhill Associates.

No, we don't have to meet or go to
the office. Most of anything can
be done remotely. Presidents solve
global issues via phone calls. So I
think we also have a chance.

Thanks but not for me.

Victoria Skurnick
vskurnick@lgrliterary.com

Thank you! It is the best rejection, no joke. I prefer it this way. No need to write an essay on how I suck that is also impersonal and non-explanatory of specific details. Because the industry is very subjective so don't get discouraged. Thus I don't.

Thank you for your recent query to the Denise Shannon Literary Agency. Unfortunately, we do not feel your project is right for us, but we wish you the best of luck elsewhere.

An agent's job is to know how to sell the book and who to sell it to for the highest price, but not feel. It's like the FBI would say they feel like the murderer is that guy instead of facts.

SKLA is experiencing irregularities with our
email system this week — if you think that you
missed an email from me, you are very likely
right!
Thanks for your patience and please do let me
know if you encounter any issues receiving messages from me.

Best,
Laura

--

Laura Usselman
Stuart Krichevsky Literary Agency, Inc.
6 East 39th Street, Suite 500
www.skagency.com

I always talk to the TV while
watching the news. That is
my civic participation.

Dear Mila,

Thank you so much for thinking of Nelson Literary Agency for your submission. Unfortunately, it's not quite what I'm looking for at the moment. I wish I could offer a more personalized response, but do know that we read every query letter and sample we receive. Even though your project is not right for us, it might be right for another agent, so don't give up! Good luck with all your publishing endeavors.

Sincerely,
Joanna MacKenzie

When you buy your first trench coat, you can't understand how you lived without one before.

Dear Mila,

I'm sorry, but your project is not a perfect
fit for me at this time. Unfortunately, I will
have to pass. Thank you for considering me and
best of luck with your future queries.

Sincerely,
Beth Marshea
Ladderbird Literary Agency

Company culture, drinking culture,
cancel culture. Doesn't it feel
like if "culture" is added, the
word next to it gets ruined?

Dear Mila,

Thanks so much for contacting me about your
book project, but I'm afraid I wouldn't be the
best representative for it. Best of luck on
your path to publication.

Sincerely,
Kate Garrick
Salky Literary Management

I'm not afraid of a nuclear war.
It's just bam, and that is it —
the end. What I'm afraid of is the
government fucking it up, and then
the unknown chaos of a completely
new unimaginable level happens —
and that is very scary.

Dear Mila,

Thank you for submitting TEN MYRIAD MOVES to me. Unfortunately, I will not be pursuing representation on this project.

Publishing is a subjective business, and other agents will surely feel differently. I sincerely wish you all the best in your search for representation and publication.

Best,
Jessica

Jessica Mileo
InkWell Management
521 Fifth Avenue, Suite 2600
New York, NY 10175
Twitter: @jessicamileo // @InkWellmgmt

One of my useless skills: fake-laughing and saying, "That's wild!" when I couldn't hear what someone said.

Hello, and thank you for the opportunity to review your work. I'm afraid the project isn't a good fit for me, but I wish you all the best in finding representation elsewhere.

All best,
Rachel Beck
Literary Agent
Liza Dawson Associates

More often than not, Italian restaurants don't have bars because Italia is all about the family, and the family sits at the table. If you're at the table, you're a part of the family. Sometimes, there's a bar at the entrance — for visitors to watch and observe.

Dear Author,

Thank you for your submission, which we look forward to reading. Please note that due to the extremely high number of queries which we receive, we will only respond if we are interested.
For further information, please consult our website, www.parkfine.com.

Please note the following exception: Peter Knapp responds to all middle grade and young adult queries, typically within about 16 weeks of receipt.

Thank you for the chance to consider your work.

Best of luck,
Park & Fine Literary and Media

The spinner ring, that's supposed to reduce anxiety, is driving me crazy!

111

Thank you for contacting **Ayesha Pande Literary**. Due to the volume of queries, agents are only able to respond if they wish to read a submission. If you have not heard back from us within 6-8 weeks, we encourage you to re-submit your story to a different agent.

As a kind reminder, please note that Ayesha Pande, Stephany Evans, Annie Hwang, and Anjali Singh are currently closed to queries.

Best regards,
Ayesha Pande Literary

--
Ayesha Pande Literary.
pandeliterary.com.
212.283.5825

Now I get why American bedding sets have a flat sheet instead of a duvet cover: nobody can fit the duvet in the duvet cover! Hashtag bestcountryintheworld.

Dear Mila,

Thank you for thinking of me for TEN MYRIAD
MOVES. I'm sorry, but your project does not
sound like a fit for me at this time, and so I
will have to pass. Nevertheless I appreciate
the chance to consider it and I hope this
project finds its way to the right agent soon.
Thanks again and all the best with your
queries!

Best,
Ismita Hussain

Alright, Sephora, assist me.
I'm looking for a moisturizer
that hides that I hate
everybody today.

Automatic reply: Query Katie Fulford

Thank you for considering Bell Lomax Moreton for your submission.

We do understand the time and effort that goes into crafting a submission, but due to the sheer volume we receive each day we are unable to give a further reply unless we want to read or hear more.

If we are interested, you will receive a response within **eight to twelve weeks** from submission.

Warmest Wishes,

The Submissions Team

CORRUPTION. The sellable term is lobbying.

114

Thank you for thinking to query me with your project. Unfortunately, it doesn't seem like a good fit for my list at this time. Again, thank you, and best of luck finding an agent.

Best,
Alexandra Machinist
alexandra.machinist@icmpartners.com

NOTE: This message contains information which may be confidential and/or privileged. It is intended solely for the addressee. If you are not the intended recipient, you may not use, copy, distribute, or disclose any information contained in the message. If you have received this transmission in error, please notify the sender by reply e-mail and delete this message. Please note, all rights of concurrent review and comment are hereby reserved. Thank you.

ICM Partners
10250 Constellation Boulevard,
Los Angeles, CA 90067 (TA000229129)
65 E. 55th Street,
New York, NY 10022 (1474108-DCA)

Giving a blunt opinion about someone, $100 for a 10-min sesh, sounds like a fun side gig. Did I just come up with a cool business idea?

Thanks so much for sending us your query. We generally respond to queries we are interested in within 12-15 weeks, although we do get behind occasionally. We're not able to respond to each query with detailed feedback, but we do appreciate your hard work and wish you the best of success with your writing career.

--

Tanenbaum International Literary Agency
tanenbauminternational.com

Sometimes I contact a company I like just to thank them for their great product or service. Robots, however, deprive me of this opportunity. Chatbots and AI can't appreciate sincerely. Their developers haven't thought this option through. Bring people back!

Thank you for your submission! If we feel your work is a good fit, our agents will respond to you within 30 days.

--

This e-mail was sent from a form on Trident Media Group (https://www.tridentmediagroup.com)

Love is like choosing a custom ring: you've been fantasizing about it for a long time, you know what kind it should be, you even have a plan B in case you don't find exactly what you're looking for soon. But then you see it at a store in a small town that you went to on a Monday afternoon because you were bored. It's not the one you thought you always wanted. You take it anyway. And it's perfect.

Thank you for your enthusiasm to submit to our agency. With much consideration, I will be closing to submissions indefinitely to focus on my current client list and will only be reviewing projects on a referral basis. Please refer to our agency website for KC&A agents currently accepting submissions. https://www.kimberley-cameron.com

I wish you luck on your publishing journey!

Sincerely,
Kimberley Cameron
kimberley@kimberleycameron.com

Complete equilibrium is when nothing is happening at all.

118

Dear Mila,

Unfortunately, your query does not meet our particular need at this time, but thank you for giving us the chance to review your work. Good luck in future.

Barbara Bova Literary Agency LLC
http://www.barbarabovaliteraryagency.com

There are two places in New York City where you can cry publicly without being bothered: the subway and a massage table at physical therapy.

Dear Mila,

Thanks for your query. Due to the huge stack of manuscripts awaiting my review, I must declare a moratorium on new submissions for the next six months. I appreciate your thinking of JET Literary Associates and I wish you every success with your work.

Cordially,
Liz Trupin-Pulli

I was waiting for the elevator and saw through the window a kindergarten in the building across. Kids were playing and the whole room was filled with pure joy. The scene gave hope. I saw hope. Children are our hope. Well, that's a weird PMS this month.

Attn. Mila Ilkova

We received your query submitted to Mollie Glick inquiring about having Creative Artists Agency consider the query letter for above-entitled project. Although we appreciate your interest, we are not able to move forward with your query at this time.

Your query letter has not been, and will not be disclosed to any executive or other employee of Creative Artists Agency or any other person. You should be aware that many ideas are generated by our employees and our clients or other sources.

Thank you for taking the time to submit your query and considering Creative Artists Agency. We wish you much luck in your endeavors.

Cordially,

Creative Artists Agency

A relationship based only on casual sex is like shearing a pig — a lot of squealing but zero wool.

Thank you for your query. It has been received, and we look forward to reading your work. Unfortunately, due to the current volume of submissions, we are not able to respond personally to everyone. If one of our agents is interested in your project they will be in touch within 6 to 8 weeks.

--

Waxman Literary Agency
www.waxmanliteraryagency.com

Eat right — your body is a temple. But sometimes, you want to turn it into a crack house and shove a greasy burger into it.

Dear Ms. Ilkova

Thank you for your email describing your manuscript.

Unfortunately, due to my backlog and a very full and stable list, I am not taking on any new work for the foreseeable future.

I am sorry, thank you for thinking of me, and I wish you success in finding an agent and/or editor that will help you achieve publication.

Sincerely
Cherry Weiner
Cherry Weiner Literary Agency

I had Instagram for a total of 12 minutes. It synced my contacts, but instead, it kept suggesting I follow all of the Kardashians. There're so many of them! I couldn't. I just couldn't.

Dear querying writers: I am off until November 28. If you have not heard back from me by November 30, 2022, I am not interested in your project, but I wish you all the best with it and thank you for thinking of me.
My best,
Uwe
uwe@triadaus.com

It's time to relax and watch some Netflix. "WARNING: Nudity, sex, language, violence..." Perfect. I don't watch a movie without all that.

THIS IS AN AUTO REPLY. Thank you for your interest in P.S. Literary Agency. We have received your e-mail and your query will be reviewed shortly.

If we are interested in seeing further material we normally respond within 4-6 weeks. If you have not heard from us after 4-6 weeks, you may assume we have reviewed your query and determined that your project is not the best fit for our agency.

To learn more about our Submission Guidelines, please check our submissions page: http://www.psliterary.com/submissions

Thanks again for your interest!

Sincerely,
P.S. Literary Agency

NOTE: Please do not send e-mail attachments unless specifically requested by us.

****THIS IS AN AUTO REPLY****

Envy and conscience are the 24-hour guards. Envy comes during the day and conscience at night.

Thank you for querying MacKenzie Wolf.

Due to the very high volume of queries we receive we are not able to respond to every message.

Please allow up to twelve weeks for an interested agent to respond directly.

Please note that as of February 15th, 2021 Rach Crawford will no longer be accepting emailed queries. (Queries recieved by email before this date will still be considered.) You can query her via the online form at http://QueryManager.com/rachac

All politicians are the same.
It's like the circus opened a
franchise worldwide.

Thank you for your submission to Capital Talent Agency's literary division. If we are interested in pursuing an agency relationship with you, we will endeavor to contact you within six weeks of your query or submission.

On abortion rights.

Men, imagine a small group of women telling you never to touch your penis. No, not even once, not even if it's an emergency or a life-threatening situation (if only there were one involving a penis). And you can't touch your balls either. Take your hand off your balls because they create the future form of a fetus. Do you want to be in charge of your own body? Ha! What? You touch your balls — you touch children. Pedophile!

121

Dear Mila,

Thank you for your email! Unfortunately I am
not open to queries. My client list is very
full at the moment, and I'm not able to take on
anyone new at this time. I wish you the best of
luck!

Sincerely,
--
Erin C. Niumata
F O L I O Literary Management, LLC
630 9th Avenue, Suite 1101
New York, NY 10036
www.foliolit.com
212-400-1494 ext 280

On abortion rights 2.
Instead of banning abortion after
6 weeks, pay women for each kid as
they do in Russia — a maternity
fund. And add a fully paid 1-year
maternity leave. This way, women will
feel financially secure to give birth.
No joke.

Philip Spitzer passed away in October of 2021. The agency he founded lives on, however, with his daughter Anne-Lise Spitzer as EVP.

To reach Anne-Lise with submissions and introductions: annelise.spitzer@spitzeragency.com

To reach Lukas Ortiz for foreign rights, subrights and all other rights questions: lukas.ortiz@spitzeragency.com

For all other business, fanmail, requests and permissions, email: kim.lombardini@spitzeragency.com

We look forward to hearing from you.

Kim

Ah, they started to die.

129

Thank you very much for your email.

Due to the volume of queries we receive, I am only able to respond if I am interested in seeing more material, in which case I will contact you within four weeks.

I appreciate your patience, and for thinking of the Aaron Priest Literary Agency.

Anyone who will figure out how to sell that rare feeling of goosebumps (through a product or a service) will be the richest person alive. Robots can do better all the rest.

Thank you for your message. I am no longer at
ESA, so please be in touch with
Margaret Sutherland Brown at <u>margaret@em-</u>
<u>masweeneyagency,com</u> with any inquiries.
Best wishes,
Kira

Manuscript wishlist: "Fiction and non-fiction projects that make people fall in love with reading — through beautiful writing, dynamic characters, and engaging plots. Visceral comfort reads that remind of M.T. Anderson's Feed for the TikTok generation, climate utopias with cyberpunk multinational features and innovative space opera adventures that shine a spotlight on people and places, and start new conversations. Whatever the age group, I tend to love contrast-highbrow sentences and lowbrow content, beautiful settings and ugly motives — the books that are

131

these sound like fun boks, but not like the right fit for my list, so will alas, good-naturedly decline.

--

Felicia Eth
FELICIA ETH LITERARY REPRESENTATION
FeliciaEth.Literary@Gmail.com
www.ethliterary.com
415-970-0717

beautiful and scary, heartbreaking and hilarious. I love secrets, scheming, revenge, plotting, and stories that have to be written forward and backward to make sense (I LOVE discovering a very cleverly planted clue that makes sense in retrospect). I love watching powerful people navigate their public and private lives. But if the voice is wonderful, I can love just about anything."

Facepalm, eye-roll, poop emoji, poop emoji, poop emoji.

I am closed to unsolicited submissions. Please query one of my colleagues at Fuse Literary. Directions are on our website.

Laurie McLean, Partner
FUSE LITERARY
laurie@fuseliterary.com
fuseliterary.com
she/her

A dead funny idea for a movie: a character who's trying to kill himself but constantly chooses the wrong ways: drinking tap water to poison himself or using plastic knives to cut wrists, trying to drown himself in a kiddie pool or hang himself with a clothes hanger, trying to drown in an extra large soda cup in cinema or hang himself with a Christmas tinsel. And, finally, overdosing on vitamin B.

133

Thank you so much for your query! We are excited to read your pages.

Please allow eight weeks to read each pitch. Due to the high volume of submissions we receive, we cannot respond individually to every single email. We will reach out if we are interested in reading more: if you do not hear from us after eight weeks, we are not the best fit for this project.

We look forward to reading!
Best,
Rebecca Friedman Literary

Men's approach to life: I wake up and piss excellence.
Woman's approach to life: what am I doing wrong today — not slim enough, not smiley enough, not glowy enough?

AUTO-RESPONSE

This confirms our receipt of your email.
Please see below or visit our website to see
changes to our Query process.
We will only reply to queries if we are interested in reading more/reading the full manuscript. We want to have a faster response time
to your query and plan on responding to queries
we're
ceipt
to le
throu
    If
from
know
query
the d
    We
commu
Auto-

    --

Brower Literary & Management
Mailing Address: 13720 Old St. Augustine Rd.,
Ste 8-512, Jacksonville, FL 32258
phone: 646.854.6073
website: http://browerliterary.com/

Thank you for your interest in querying
Browne & Miller Literary Associates about your
book project. However, we are currently closed
to queries until the end of February 2023
(please check our social media for exact
date). We will update our website when the inbox has re-opened, and invite you to try us
again then.

Browne & Miller is ~~NOT~~ rently seeking:
Adult and Mid-
re fantasy nov-
tories; screen-
d in previously
or series, or

Good pen.

I'm taking it.

query process,

p

/

pes of projects
we are seeking, please visit:
www.publishersmarketplace.com/members/mpdinc/
and
www.manuscriptwishlist.com/mswl-post/
danielle-egan-miller/

Thanks again for your interest,
Team BMLA

136

Dear Mila,

Thank you for giving me the opportunity to consider representing TEN MYRIAD MOVES.

Unfortunately, I've decided to pass on this book.

After a great amount of consideration, I've made the difficult decision to reduce the amount of new work that I take on at this time. My client list has grown and become very full, which consumes most of my work time. Also, the literary market is increasingly tight, making it difficult to place manuscripts. So, regretfully, I'm not taking on any new work.

I encourage you to send your manuscripts to other agents, so that they can receive the attention they deserve.

I appreciate your interest in my agency. I wish you the very best with TEN MYRIAD MOVES and success in publishing your work.

Sincerely,

Pam

--
Pamela Hopkins
Literary Agent
Hopkins Literary Associates
hlasubmissions@gmail.com

This line looks like death on a defibrillator.

137

Sorry, not taking on new clients at the moment.

peter@fineprintlit.com

"If you were inside of me, aka home, you'd be so warm and moisturized with my cum that this week wouldn't seem so cold. Because nothing feels like hole, I mean home."

and send...

Oh god, oh god, oh god! I typed the wrong message into the wrong message! Obviously, I didn't mean to send a query letter like this. I did not! I so did not! Would it help though?... Erh, too late.

Thank you for your email. This message confirms my receipt of your query. Due to the
large number of submissions I receive, I can no
longer guarantee a response. I will only respond if I would like to read your manuscript,
but please be assured that your query will be
read. I appreciate receiving submissions from
writers who I haven't had the chance to meet.

If I have met you in person (or virtually) at
a writers conference or book event we both at-
tended, or if you are coming to me through an
author I represent or through a mutual friend
or colleague, please email your query to Tamara
Kawar at tamara@defliterary.com directly and
let me know the connection in your query.
Please also put "Query referral for Miriam Altshuler" in the subject line of your email.

Many thanks for the opportunity to consider
your work.

Cordially,
Miriam Altshuler
DeFiore and Company

I want to write a poem
about annoyance,
but can't find a rhyme
to 12 exclamation points.

139

Hello, Mila,

Thanks for sharing your queries with us, but your novels don't seem to be the style that we are familiar with, or that works for us. Sorry to disappoint you.

Dave Fessenden, for WordWise Media

Not familiar with humor?
Life must be hard.

Hello,

Thank you for the chance to read your work. Unfortunately, we are not the best fit for this piece at this time, and we wish you the absolute best in placing it elsewhere.

Best Regards,
Vicky Bijur Literary Agency

Maybe I should start looking for work... Wait a minute...more submissions?! Ugh, fuck me!

141

I'm so sorry but I'm not an agent anymore. Good luck elsewhere though!

Best,
Amy Tipton

Job posting somewhere online: "To apply, please email an interesting (meaning, not copy pasted, boring or typical) cover letter and your resume. Seamlessly include the words "platypus" and "enigma" somewhere in your cover letter or resume. Really. We want it to reflect who you are and how you engage in the world." Platypus and enigma... Seamlessly...aha.

Dear Mila Ilkova,

Thank you for submitting to Regina Ryan Books. Unfortunately, our office does not handle works of fiction.

We wish you the best of luck with your novel nevertheless.

Raina Mansfield,
Assistant to Regina Ryan
Regina Ryan Books

As it turns out, the New York Department of Labor handles only unemployment. The last time they provided work for someone was when smoking in the office was allowed. They could call themselves the Department of Unemployment; or serve free sandwiches — same thing.

Sorry not agenting.

Hope this helps.

Cheers,

Mike

Michael Larsen Author Coaching
Free coaching for qualified writers
of books about change. Info at:
michaellarsenauthorcoaching.com

How to Write a Book Proposal, 5th Edition, by
Jody Rein with Michael Larsen
How to Get a Literary Agent (3rd edition)
Guerrilla Marketing for Authors: 100 Weapons
for Selling Your Work (coauthor) (2nd edition)
Writing Success Guaranteed: How to Build a
Career Doing What You Love (In progress)

So many people write all kinds of how—tos but only a few actually know how to and just do it.

No longer accepting queries.

Jon Tienstra
722 Hogan Drive
Martinsburg WV
25405

610-737-7112

Talking to an alconaut is like explaining philosophy to a retarded person. He listens to you attentively, nods along, and then saliva involuntarily flows from his mouth, and you realize that all the talk is in vain.

145

Hi, Mila,

Thank you for sending this along. I read your letter with interest, but I'm afraid the concept for the series feels outside my wheelhouse and so, I'm afraid I'm going to pass. I do appreciate you sharing this with me and I wish you every success!

Regards,

Gina Panettieri, Founder
Talcott Notch Literary Services, LLC
215 Broad Street, 2nd floor
Milford, Connecticut 06460
203.876.4959

Recent and notable
BLUE LIKE ME by Aaron Philip Clark (Thomas & Mercer)
SONS OF VALOR by Andrews & Wilson (Blackstone Publishing)
HITMEN by Scott Deitche (Rowman & Littlefield)
THE WEDDING PLOT by Paula Munier (Minotaur)

Everyone starts off as a perfectionist, but your standards diminish over the years.

Dear Writer:

I am currently closed to queries. Your submission will not be reviewed.

I am sorry for this auto-response, but I sim-
ply need to take a break to get caught up.

All best,
Barry Goldblatt

When someone from the past suddenly texts: "I'm thinking about you," what the hell am I supposed to do with this information, huh? Keep your thoughts to yourself. I've got enough of my own. The past should stay in the past.

Thank you for sharing your work with us at the Mendel Media Group. This automatically generated email is confirmation of its arrival. If we feel we can represent your work and want to discuss it further, we will email or call you directly. If not, we won't respond further. As we can't respond personally to every submission, please don't interpret a lack of response to your work (beyond this email) as a judgment about its merit. We can not, unfortunately, take on every worthy project sent to us.

Keep writing!
Mendel Media Group LLC

The speed of eating one crepe is exactly twice faster than making one crepe.

148

Thank you for your message!

I no longer work at the Beth Vesel Literary Agency. For further assistance, please contact Callie Deitrick at callie.deitrick@bvlit.com or Beth Vesel at beth.vesel@bvlit.com.

Best,
Greta

--

Greta Moran, Associate Agent
Beth Vesel Literary Agency
202 Riverside Drive, Suite 9B
New York, New York 10025
http://www.bvlit.com
+1 (917) 405-8270

Bank notification: "Do you need help spending only what you have in your account?"
I can spend all of the accounts you have, bank. Give me the passwords and get ready for the party.

149

Dear Mila,

Thank you so much for your interest in the
Jennifer Lyons Literary Agency. We are sorry to
tell you that we have decided to pass on your
project.

We wish you the best of luck,
The Jennifer Lyons Literary Agency
jenniferlyonsagency2@gmail.com

As a grown-up woman, there
is nothing I can not do. Well,
there's a lot I can not do, but
there's nothing I can not do.

Dear Author,

Thank you for your submission. Your work has been carefully reviewed by the agent you queried, and it has been determined that Holloway Literary will not be pursuing representation of your manuscript. We regret sending you this information in a form letter; however, due to the volume of emails we receive daily it is almost impossible to send customized letters to every author. Thank you again for thinking of Holloway Literary, and we wish you every success in your writing career.

Best,
Brianna Summers, Submissions Coordinator
Holloway Literary
www.HollowayLiterary.com

Please note our new email address submissions@hollowayliterary.com

Am I old enough to say "God, I hate technology!"? Because I do! I really do!

151

Your message to jennifer@jenniferlyonsliter-aryagency.com couldn't be delivered.

jennifer wasn't found at jenniferlyonsliter-aryagency.com.

Apparently, I applied to 273 jobs on LinkedIn. No responses. The White House would respond faster. I mean, it did, unlike an LLC in NYC.

Dear Sender, this mailbox is no longer in
use. Please remove this address from your mailing lists. If you do not have an alternate contact, please reach out to us by phone at (312)
922-3063

Abby Saul
abbies@browneandmiller.com

You know you've lived
about half of your life
when you start coughing
after intense laughter.

As stated in my bio on the Rees Agency's website, I'm permanently closed to queries.

Ann Collette
Rees Literary Agency
@Ann_Collette

The Social Science Research Council
(SSRC) is a Brooklyn, NY-based, in-
dependent, international, nonprofit
organization devoted to the ad-
vancement of interdisciplinary research in the social sciences and
related disciplines through a wide
variety of workshops and conferences, fellowships and grants,
summer training institutes, schol-
arly exchanges, research, and
publications. Sounds like the perfect
organization for money laundering.

Thank you for your query. If we are interested in seeing more we will contact you with in 4-6 weeks.

If you don't hear from us, we will not be pursuing. Thank you and best wishes.

--
The Elizabeth Kaplan Literary Agency
138 West 25th Street
Suite 1D
New York, NY 10001
(212) 255-5117

The building Grace in NYC looks so not graceful.

Loretta Barrett Books, Inc. no longer accepts submissions. Please direct your query to the Vertical Ink Agency at VIAQuery@gmail.com. Thank you.

--
Loretta Barrett Books, Inc.
170 Union Street, Suite 4L
Brooklyn, NY 11231
212-242-3420
www.lorettabarrettbooks.com

There are so many people with ugly toes.

Thanks, but this does not sound right for our small agency. Good luck.

Robin Straus
Robin Straus Agency Inc.

robin@robinstrausagency.com
www.robinstrausagency.com
www.wallaceliteraryagency.com

Oh my god! A fork was killed here!

Dear Author,

Thank you for giving us the opportunity to consider your work. Due to the enormous volume of electronic submissions we receive, it is impossible to respond personally to every one. However, if we are interested in your project, you will hear back from us directly. Thanks for understanding.

Sincerely,

The VIA Team

--
Vertical Ink Agency
170 Union Street, Suite 4L
Brooklyn, NY 11231
M: 917-535-4763
http://www.vertical-ink-agency.com/

Feeling like a
star today, so
no comment.

Thank you for your message. I am out of the office visiting family, and replies will be delayed. If you have an urgent matter, please contact one of my colleagues; otherwise, I'll reply as soon as possible upon my return. I appreciate your patience.

Sincerely,
Sarah E. Younger

PS: Enjoy Super Bowl Weekend, if not for the football, for the snacks!

—

Sarah Elizabeth Younger - Senior Agent
Nancy Yost Literary Agency
www.nyliterary.com
http://www.nyliterary.com
(she/her/hers)

Pizza and a movie is actually a great Saturday night plan in New York City.

159

Thank you for contacting ESA. If you have sent us a query about your manuscript, please sit tight while we read your work. Because of the volume of e-mail we receive, we are unfortunately only able to respond to queries when we're interested in reading more. If you have an administrative question regarding the agency -- foreign rights, who we represent, etc -- please contact info@emmasweeneyagency.com Many thanks and best wishes.

Hm...a 30-year-old woman wearing a tiara... Why isn't Vogue regulating this fashion choice anyhow? Shouldn't the maximum age for a tiara be, I don't know, 9?

Due to the volume of submissions received, please note that we cannot respond to every query. We shall contact you if we wish to pursue your submission.

Janklow & Nesbit Associates

"A toothbrush station to clear counter clutter and prevent goopy messes with a wall-mounted unit that stores and dispenses the perfect amount of toothpaste on your brushes every time. It's much more sanitary than leaving out uncovered brushes AND it conveniently holds four rinse cups."
Who writes this copy for idiots?
Is anyone ever confused about the amount of toothpaste?

161

Many thanks for contacting Darhansoff & Verrill Literary Agents. Due to volume, we are no longer replying to each individual query submitted for our review. We will be in touch only if we are interested in reading your work. If you haven't heard from us within 8-10 weeks, it is safe to say that we have passed on the opportunity and wish you the best of luck elsewhere.

Which one is it? Still a No?
At least some sort of
stability in life.

162

Hi,

Thanks for querying. I am currently closed to submissions.

Best,
Liza
lizadawsonassociates.com

Henry Miller, besides writing, also did watercolors. I, besides writing, want to save all free wooden furniture from Craigslist and refinish it in a garage. I guess all businesses in America do start in a garage.

Hello,

Thank you for submitting your query! Unfortunately my query inbox is closed as of March 27th, 2020. Feel free to follow my twitter (@LightnerKayla) for updates on when I will be open again.

Best,
Kayla

--
Kayla Lightner
Liza Dawson Associates
121 W 27th Street, Suite 1201
New York, NY 10001

People are more willing to do something out of spite than out of love.

Dear Mila,

Thank you for your query! I so appreciate the opportunity to review your work, but I'm afraid that it's just not the best fit for my list at this time. Don't be discouraged, though. Publishing is a marathon, not a sprint, and you just need one person to catch that shared vision. Best of luck to you!

Whitney Ross
Irene Goodman Literary Agency
27 West 24th St. Suite 804
New York, NY 10010
www.irenegoodman.com

It all starts with 1 person doing 1 annoying thing, then a group of people do it, then a community, a city, a country, and then a whole world is full of assholes. Is that the world you want to live in? Don't be that 1 person.

165

Hello,

Thank you for your patience as I considered your query. I appreciate you trusting me with your work at this stage, but I don't feel I am the right agent for your project. I wish you all the best of luck in finding a home for your book.

Sincerely,
Ashley

--
Ashley Lopez (she/her)
Agent, Rights Manager
Waxman Literary Agency
We've moved!
11 East 44th Street
Suite 1603
New York, NY 10017
ashley@waxmanagency.com
212.675.5556

MaRRied people seNd their wishes NOt to the UNiveRse but directly to their paRtNeR.

Dear Mila,

Thanks for your query. I wish I could represent every book I enjoy. Because my resources are limited, I can only devote my energy to projects that I feel passionate about, and I'm sorry to say that your books aren't right for me.

I really appreciate being given an opportunity to consider your work, and I wish you all the best in finding the right agent and getting published.

Best wishes,
Annie Bomke
ajbomke@gmail.com

The moment I have my inner Joey Tribbiani laugh every time is when I hear the word "pussyfoot."

Thanks for sharing your query with me. I regret to inform you that I won't be requesting additional materials or offering representation.

Please know I can only responsibly take on a few new clients each year, and my decision to pass does not mean another agent won't be a passionate and energetic advocate for your project.

Please accept my very best wishes for your writing success.

Respectfully,

Kat

KATHERINE ODOM-TOMCHIN
AUDIO RIGHTS DIRECTOR / LITERARY AGENT
Folio Literary Management | Folio Jr.
630 9th Avenue, Suite 1101,
New York, NY 10036
212-400-1494 x470
ktomchin@foliolit.com | FolioLit.com

Back in the day, people said less shit because of duels.

Thank you for your recent query letter, and for affording Flannery Literary the pleasure and privilege of considering your work for representation. Please forgive us for this form letter response; a publishing shortcut we reluctantly resort to in the interest of time given how many queries we receive. Rest assured that the time we did not spend personalizing this note was instead spent carefully considering your query to assess whether or not we believed we might be the best literary agent for your work.

We are going to have to pass on the opportunity to work with you at this time; given our current workload, we are, regretfully, taking on very few new projects at the moment. Please know that we are not passing judgement on the worth or merit of your writing or your manuscript—we are a small agency, and we must pass up far more than we are able to take on.

We wish you the best of luck in your future marketing efforts. Keep going. Don't give up. Now, more than ever, the world needs good books for children and young adults. Thank you for being part of the solution which is, always and forever, bringing people, especially young people, to the edification and illumination of books. The only magic we have ever seen is what happens between the writer and the page, and the page and the reader.

We know how daunting it is to submit your writing to the scrutiny of strangers, and we appreciate the bravery it takes to send your hopes and dreams into the world. We salute your hard work and courage; Flannery Literary will forever cheer for the writers who are finding their way to their readers.

With thanks for thinking of us, and best wishes in all your publishing endeavors,

Jennifer Flannery
Flannery Literary

How to know that cheese with mold went bad and spot which mold is the one you're not supposed to eat?

169

Sorry, my list is full at the moment!
emorgen@stonesong.com

I am persuaded that there is no going back to anything. At all.

Many thanks for sending your query! I try to
respond to every query in a timely manner, so
please do re-query if you don't get a response
within two weeks. Additionally, I ask that all
queries include the first ten pages of your
book pasted into the body of the email.   If
your query did not include these pages, please
resend it and please remember to include the
original query along with the pages.

Thanks so much for trusting me with your work
and I'll be in touch soon.

Jenny Bent
The Bent Agency

Tinder:
"Hey, Mila! On a scale of 1 to
America, how free are you
tomorrow night?"
Hm...to replace 1D like that
you need to have a valid
passport and visit at least
1D countries.

111

Thanks for thinking of me, Mila, but I closed
my agency in the fall of 2018 (link https://
www.villagerexpat.com/2018/11/exploring-oppor-
tunities-in-digital-and.html).

You might find names of agents and editors to
query on the Poets & Writers magazine website.
Go to pw.org and see the Publish Your Writing
tab.

Best wishes,
Debbie Carter

Social media gave a voice
to a lot of interesting
and intellectual people.
Unfortunately, people with
a lesbian dance theory
degree from Bath Spa
And Beyond University
also got a chance to
spread their opinion.

112

Thanks so much for your query. Unfortunately, this is not a fit for my list at this time and I must pass. I wish you the very best of success in finding an enthusiastic agent.

Best,
Matt

Matt Wagner
Fresh Books, Inc.
530-344-9202

Leaving a footprint in history sounds good, whereas leaving a fingerprint for tech companies does not. A buttprint in the form of a Netflix password is what we can actually offer future generations.

<clelia@martinliterarymanagement.com>: host
aspmx.l.google.com[108.177.15.26]
said: 550-5.1.1 The email account that
you tried to reach does not exist.

Deep state, deepfake,
deep throat, deep thought,
Deep Purple. Cross out the
unnecessary.

114

Thanks so much for being in touch and sending
this along. It's not for me so I'll step aside
but thanks again and good luck with it.
All best
Nicola Barr
thebentagency.com

Sometimes getting drunk is
a part of the wellness
program in a big city.

Dear Mila,

Thank you for your email. We have reviewed your query, but unfortunately, this project is not right for our agency at this time. We encourage you to continue writing and sharing your work, and we wish you the best of luck in finding the agent who will be the right fit for your project. We appreciate you for thinking of us for this query.

Sincerely,
Ann Proust
Editorial Assistant

The Charlotte Gusay Literary Agency
Los Angeles, CA 90064
http://www.gusay.com

Maybe, just maybe, higher education is BS? They even write it that way: BS in journalism, BS in business, BS in social studies.

Hi, Mila,

Not sure how this happened, but I'm not the Craig Literary Agency that it seems you're attempting to query.

Tracy Crow
President
MilSpeak Foundation, Inc.
Tracy Crow Literary Agency

s: www.milspeakfoundation.org
s: www.tracycrow.com
p: (727) 742-8346

The social trend is complete independence from everyone and everything. But the ideal world is links of balanced dependencies. Instead, we are offered links to promo codes to buy stuff. Link me to a fabulous person, not to shoes on sale.

111

Jennifer Udden has left the Barry Goldblatt
Agency.

She is now at New Leaf Literary and can be
reached at judden@newleafliterary.com. You can
also reach out to Tricia Ready, Tricia@bgliter-
ary.com.

--

Barry Goldblatt Literary
www.bgliterary.com
320 7th Avenue #266
Brooklyn, NY 11215

@suddenlyjen
http://twitter.com/suddenlyjen
(713)303-9615
www.jenniferudden.com

PeRhaps I should tRy the bcc
technique with dating: have
the first date with multiple
men at once to save time.
It's the same questions
and answers anyway.

Hello, and thank you for your email.

I've left the BGL and have moved to join the team at New Leaf Literary & Media.

This query address is no longer operational. Thereafter you can query me by following the querying instructions for New Leaf Literary.

Thank you for your patience during this time.

All best

Jen

https://www.newleafliterary.com/submissions/

Plan for the day: perfecting the illusion "I have my shit together."

179

Thanks for your email. As of 12/5/2020 I'm no longer at New Leaf.

If you have any questions for anyone at New Leaf, please contact assist@newleafliterary.com.

All best

Jen

Spent a beautiful day with my friend on his boat "Cirrhosis of the River." It was very Cool McFool.

```
<jpulcini@jplm.com>:              host
mx1.netsolmail.net[172.65.252.97]  said:  550
5.7.1
        <jpulcini@jplm.com>... Relaying  denied
(in reply to RCPT TO command)
```

Ugh, even their host
denied my book.

181

Thank you for your message. I am currently traveling overseas and have only sporadic access to email. I will be back at the office on 02/21/23.

Best,
Sandy

--

Sandy Lu
Literary Agent
Book Wyrm Literary Agency

Good for you, Sandy! Over which sea did you go? I need a vacation too, for like 5 months, so I can sit on the beach, spread my toes and watch the seagulls shit on the go.

Hello.

Thank you for your email. I am no longer with the L. Perkins Agency but please visit www.lperkinsagency.com for information on other agents.

All the best-
L

If you say L more than 10 times, it unavoidably sounds like La. La-la-la-la-la.

183

Is this the blank email where they want to gift me $33 million and immortality, but I will never find out? The silver lining is that $33 million would be so not enough for eternity, so I'm happy with what I already have.

--
Benjamin Ickies
Development Associate
Stephen Pevner, Inc.
382 Lafayette St., 8th Floor
New York, NY 10003
212.674.8541

184

Thank you for your email. I am traveling through February 15th, 2023 with limited email access. If this is urgent please ring our office at 212-633-8811 otherwise I will reply as soon as I am able.

Bernadette Baker-Baughman
Victoria Sanders & Associates
212.633.8811
vsanders@victoriasanders.com

That is the whole point of replying: as soon as you're able to.

185

Dear Mila,

Thank you for your interest in our agency. Just to clarify, we only accept submissions in English and French. If your series is in either of those languages, please send the first three chapters of the first book our way, and our team will give it a read in the weeks to come.

Kind regards,
Hollie Partis
Susanna Lea Associates

I sent my query in English, didn't I? Not Korean, not Ukrainian, not Hindi. English. Just to clarify, the book is in English. And just to clarify again, you'll give it a read in the weeks to come, right? Not in the weeks that passed?

Thanks, sorry to report this is not a fit for
me, good luck!
--
Best,
M

"We believe your data is your priori-
ty and support your right to privacy
and transparency. Select a data
access level and duration to choose
how we use and share your data:
silver, gold, platinum, 1 month, 3
months, 1 year. Silver 1 month is the
highest level of privacy. Data ac-
cessed for necessary basic oper-
ations only. Data shared with 3rd
parties to ensure the site is secure
and works on your end."
Hey! How about don't! Don't collect
my data at all if you support my
right to privacy.

187

Hello, and thank you for your message.

If you are a querying author, please note that while I appreciate the chance to consider your work, I am currently closed to unsolicited queries. During this time, all unsolicited queries will be deleted unread. If you are emailing to inquire about the status of a query you sent **prior** to November 15, 2022, please rest assured that I will be in touch, as I answer every question I receive.

Please also note that when I am open to queries, I am only responding to those received via Query Manager. When I reopen, you can query me here: https://QueryManager.com/Lauren-Spieller

Thank you,

Lauren Spieller
Literary Agent
TriadaUS Literary Agency
triadaus.com

A woman is like ice cream: first cold, then melts, then sticks.

The Lark Group is currently closed to queries. Your email <u>will not be read</u>.

We encourage you to query us when we reopen in the Fall of 2022. Our website will say when we are reopen: http://www.larkwords.com/how-to-query/.

Thanks!

"To help protect your SkyMiles account, I will be sending you a secure Form to manually verify your SkyMiles information. Please provide the required information and click the submit button."
Would you like my DNA sample too?

Thank you for your interest!

I am currently closed to submissions (except for conferences, events, and/or anything I've agreed to remain open for), so that I can respond to everything that I currently have and/or requested. As it has always been important for me to respond to queries, I'd like a chance to do so, before opening submissions again.

Additionally, I am no longer using this email address for anything publishing-related.

Please make a note that my new email address is vicki.stormliteraryagency@gmail.com. Please direct all inquiries to my new email address.

This is an automated message.

--

Victoria A. Selvaggio
Literary Agent/Partner
Storm Literary Agency
www.stormliteraryagency.com/
www.victoriaselvaggio.com/
Facebook: www.facebook.com/vicki.selvaggio.
Twitter: @vselvaggio1
LinkedIn: www.linkedin.com/in/victoria-selvaggio-7801031b

It is a new form of perverted control when companies ask you to provide more of your data to delete your data, which they won't delete at all. Ever.

Dear Mila,

Thank you for giving us a shot at this.

We deeply regret that the demands on our time are such that we are unable to represent your project.

We wish you every success. We also hope you are and remain well in these challenging times.

Best wishes,
Claire Dippel
Assistant to Luke Janklow

Things will turn out well,
even during tough times.

Dear Mila,

Thank you so much for querying BookEnds and for giving me the opportunity to review TEN MYRIAD MOVES. I did read your letter and am going to pass on looking at further material.

I'm sorry I don't have better news. I am lucky to have a full and active client list and for that reason, I've become very particular about taking on new clients. This is by no means a criticism of your work. It's quite possible you'll find someone else who feels differently. I encourage you to keep querying and even consider other BookEnds agents for your work.

I wish you all the best in your search for representation and thank you again for giving BookEnds the opportunity.

Best,
Jessica Faust, President
BookEnds, A Literary Agency
P: 908.604.2652
www.bookendsliterary.com
@BookEndsJessica
https://youtube.com/BookEndsLiteraryAgency

I REJECT REJECTION.

Thank you for your email. I am on maternity leave until mid-July 2023 and will not be checking email.

If you need assistance during this time, please contact Ellen Scott at escott@dblackagency.com, and she'll be able to help you.

Please note I am currently closed to queries.

I look forward to connecting when I am back this summer!

Best,

SEFS

Out of all problems that the world is going through right now there's a very serious one that nobody wants to fix — comfortable yet stylish shoes that don't cost fuckedupliard dollars.

193

Dear Mila,

I'm sorry, but your project does not sound like a fit for me at this time, and so I will have to pass. Thank you for considering me and best of luck with your future queries.

Sincerely,

Chelene

When you see a woman's choice and think "Girl, you can do better," know that she can, but she's so tired of doing.

Mila, thank you for sharing your stories with us.
We'll pass.

Steven Hutson
Literary Agent, Member AALA

WORDWISE MEDIA SERVICES
4083 Avenue L, Suite 255
Lancaster, CA 93536
www.wordwisemedia.com

My stories? It's not an AA meeting to share stories. How about calling things what they really are? Not "stories". Not "writing project". Not "creative aspiration". Novel. And it's my 5th one.

195

Thanks for your email. I am out of the office traveling on business through February 14th. I will be checking email infrequently and will be back to you when I am back in the office on Wednesday, February 15th.

Thanks,
Kevan

Marsal Lyon Literary Agency
cell phone - 858-922-6087

Tampons and diapers in drugstores
are placed on shelves
opposite each other
because sometimes things can go
one way or the other.

You obviously sent this to the wrong address. I am not kelly and this isn't ktliterary.com. Please remove The Rudy Agency from your list.

What just happened? Did the agency ban me? Oh no! How can I possibly get published now that the (which one is it?) The Rudy Agency asked me to remove it from my list. But hey, Rudy, thanks for the idea. From now on, I will market my new book as "banned in the United States."

197

This email account is closed and all queries will be automatically deleted. When Louise Fury is open to queries, it is via this link: https://querymanager.com/query/LouiseFury

In the meantime, please consider checking The Bent Agency website to see who is open to queries and might be a good fit. www.thebentagency.com

Thank you!

Tinder:
"Mila, when can I eat your 🍑 — 🍑?"

Hahaha. That's not how my anatomy looks. Only 1 peach.

Dear Mila,

I'm so sorry for the slow response. I'm afraid these projects aren't a good fit for me, but thanks very much for the look! I hope you find an agent who can be the right advocate for them.

Best of luck,
Victoria

Victoria Doherty Munro
Writers House LLC
120 Broadway, 22nd Floor
New York, NY 10271
e: vdoherty@writershouse.com
t: 212-685-2400

Was she promoted to an agent?
I think she used to be Dan
Lazar's assistant before.

I'm away until November 28th with limited access to email, but I'll respond when I return. Thanks.

jenndec@aol.com

"Hello Mila,
Please tell us what you're planning to use your Wise account for. We can only get started with your transfer(s) once we've accepted your account purpose. This is to ensure that Wise is safe and secure for everyone on it. The account purpose can be submitted here."
You're money transfers app! What's the other option on the money transfers app besides money transfers? Fine, my account purpose is to be pretty.

I'm traveling for AWP through Friday, March 10, so I will be slower to respond on email. Please try my cell for anything time-sensitive.

All best,
Stephanie
sdelman@trellisliterary.com

I travelled to the Red Wings store to try the 8-inch boots cause they looked cool in the pictures online. (Going from UES to Garment district is sort of considered traveling these days). Apparently they only produce those for men, and the smallest men's size is still too big. I don't know why they don't make the 8-inch boots for women, especially when most ladies are very much fond of 8 inches.

I will be out of the office until Monday, March 20th. I will be sure to answer your message upon my return.

Best Regards,
Reilly Conlon, Associate
associate@gurmanagency.com
Gurman Agency LLC
14 Penn Plaza, Suite 1407,
New York, NY 10122-1405
Tel: 212 749 4618
www.gurmanagency.com

And then they never answer any messages. Ever. Only automated promises. I wish there were at least 1 automated response that was somewhat creative, like: "Hey, I am drowning in emails and probably won't answer you, but I'm sure you are great."

202

I am out of the office today. I'll be back to you.

Be Safe and Be Well.
Moses

Amen, Moses. I will only wait for 40 years.

I will be traveling until March 20 and will be checking my e-mails only intermittently during this time. My apologies for any delays in responding.

eric@myersliterary.com

90% of anything is absolute nonsense.

Thank you for thinking to query me with your project. Unfortunately, it doesn't seem like a good fit for my list at this time. Again, thank you, and best of luck finding an agent.

Best,
Alexandra Machinist
alexandra.machinist@caa.com

How many rejections did famous writers get before they were published? JK Rowling — rejected 14 times, Stephen King — rejected by 30 publishers, Margaret Mitchell's "Gone with the Wind" — rejected 38 times, Scott Fitzgerald — 122 rejections. I WON.

Hi Mila - Thank you so much for contacting me about representation. Unfortunately, I don't think your book would be quite right for my list at this time. Publishing is very subjective, of course, and I'm sure another agent will feel differently. Thank you for thinking of Writers House. I wish you all the best of luck with this project.

Best wishes,
Stacy

Stacy Testa
Literary Agent
Writers House
120 Broadway, 22nd Floor
New York, NY 10271
(212) 685-2400

How could I possibly think that Vince slip-ons are the best? They are so not! In need of good support, at least from my sneakers.

Thank you for your submission. We read every submission made to us, and aim to respond within 10 to 12 weeks.

Thank you, Mila

Thank you for sharing your work with us. We will read your material as quickly as possible and you should hear from us within six to eight weeks, though during busy periods it may take up twelve weeks for us to respond to your submission. Make sure you save our email address (cbcsubmissions@curtisbrown.co.uk) to your contacts list to make sure none of our future emails disappear into your spam folders. If you receive an offer of representation before you have heard from us, please make sure to let us know. If you are keen to find out more about what we do and pick up tips on writing from agents, authors and publishers check out the Curtis Brown Creative Blog, or find out about our novel writing & editing courses from our Writing School.

So 10 to 12 weeks or 6 to 8? Can't decide, just like with abortion?

201

Auto Response from <u>julie.gwinn@yahoo.com</u>

Thank you for your email. I am out of the office for the Thanksgiving holiday but will respond to your email the following week.

For the whole day, I've been singing a radio commercial from 2001 promoting Kashtan Electronics — a store that sold washing machines, fridges, and vacuum cleaners. Human memory works in mysterious ways.

208

Hello,

I will be out of the office until Wednesday, October 12th.
For any urgent questions, please reach out to Julie Flanagan (julie.flanagan@caa.com).

All best,
Estie Berkowitz

A—a—achoo!

Following CAA's Acquisition of ICM Partners, CAA Agents, including former ICM Agents, now operate under CAA. This e-mail and any files transmitted with it are intended solely for the use of the individual or entity to whom they are addressed. If the reader of this e-mail is not the intended recipient or the employee or agent responsible for delivering the message to the intended recipient, you are hereby notified that any use dissemination, forwarding, printing or copying of this e-mail is strictly prohibited. CAA is committed to ensuring that clients are free to do their best work without experiencing harassment and want to ensure they have the relevant resources they need. Clients can go to https://www.caa.com/legal/sexual-harassment-guidelines-caa-clients to learn more about their rights, and how to report violations.

In performing services for you, we regularly receive, process and maintain certain personal information about you. For information about how Creative Artists Agency, LLC and its subsidiaries process such personal data, please see our Privacy Notice https://www.caa.com/legal/client-privacy-notice.

209

Automatic reply from <u>arielle@dclagency.com</u>:

    I am out of the office this week, only occasionally checking email. I will return Monday, February 13.
    Best,
    Arielle

It's cloudy in NYC, northeast wind, probability of the world falling apart 10–35%, feels like 92–147%

Thank you for reaching out to us!
- If you are submitting a query, please use our new form at Query Manager.
- If you are following up on a query you've already submitted, one of us will get back to you.

All the best,
Handspun Literary

--
Handspun Literary Agency, Inc.
www.handspunlit.com
@handspunlit

Mom's visiting. It took her a while to figure out streets and avenues in New York City. But even with zero English, she became very good at sign navigation. Her favorite street is One Way.

211

Dear Mila,

Thanks very much for trusting me with your work. I appreciate the opportunity to take a look at TEN MYRIAD MOVES, but unfortunately it doesn't seem like a good fit for my list at this time.
Of course this business is nothing if not subjective, so I have no doubt you'll find enthusiastic representation elsewhere.
Thank you for considering me & best of luck with your future queries.

Sincerely,
Justin Brouckaert

Mom shared a life hack: drinking tomato juice after vodka won't make you drunk. 2 interesting facts I didn't know — this and that my mom knows this. And I don't even drink vodka. Well, now I want to, for the sake of experiment.

Dear Mila,

Thank you for your interest in The Rosenberg Group. Please know that I appreciate and respect the time and effort you have put into crafting TEN MYRIAD MOVES. I'd like to respond in a more personal manner, but the volume of submissions I receive doesn't permit me to do so. I have read your query letter am sorry to write that this will be a pass for me.

Sincerely,

Barbara Collins Rosenberg
@RosenbergLit

Mom and I watched Avatar 2. After the hunting scene, she said: "So, when Americans watch this movie, who do they support — their fellow Americans, who are killing avatars for money or avatars?

I think you meant this for Miriam Altshuler at DeFiore, as her name/email address appears in the "to" part of the email. If not, please know it's not a commonly accepted practice to send out a mass query that is not personalized for each agent.

But since you sent this to me, I took a look and unfortunately this is not a project for me. Of course this is a subjective opinion, but I can only respond affirmatively to projects that personally appeal to me and that I can see taking to market successfully.

Wishing you much success.

Best regards,
****
Darlene Chan
Agent
www.lindachester.com
darlene@lindachester.com

Mom recently entered the new stage of her life called Medicare and started calling everyone 2 nicknames — junkie and prostitute. And if we all copy our parents at some point — I can't wait.

Thank you for your email. I'm out of the office from March 2nd until March 14th with no access to email. I'll respond to your message as soon as I can upon my return on Wednesday, March 15th. If you need something urgently, please contact Adam Reed at adam@joyharrisliterary.com.

Very best,
Alice

--

Alice Fugate
The Joy Harris Literary Agency, inc.
1501 Broadway Suite 2605
New York, New York 10036
alice@joyharrisliterary.com
www.joyharrisliterary.com

I've noticed that a guy who works in the movie industry in NYC is always chubby and bald.

Automatic reply from <u>jdarga@aevitascreative.-</u>
<u>com</u>:

Thank you for your email. I am back in the
office and going through email -- I aim to get
back to everyone by EOD Friday.

Once, a female friend of mine had a fight with a conflictology pro-fessor, won the arguments, elimi-nated contradictions, resolved the conflict, and left with dignity. And he was the one with a PhD.

Automatic reply: Query comedy/contemporary fiction 75,000 words
From dwilliams@writershouse.com

So just blank, huh?

211

Fairbank Literary is at the Bologna Book Fair and will not be replying to queries until April 2023.

A year later, they are still at the book fair. Oh my god! I've wasted a year of my life on querying...

```
MAILER-DAEMON@mail159c38.carrierzone.com
Returned mail: see transcript for details
The original message was received at Mon, 13
Feb 2023 14:43:39 -0500
from mail-40137.protonmail.ch [185.70.40.137]

        ----- The following addresses had perma-
nent fatal errors -----
    \christopher.stuartagency.com
        (expanded from: \christopher.stuarta-
gency.com)

        ----- Transcript of session follows -----
552 5.2.2 User's mailbox is full
```

I agree. It was a fatal error sending personalized (in the beginning) emails to strangers.

Automatic reply from jane@dystel.com

I am out of the office on vacation and will be back on February 15th. If you have an emergency, please me in touch with Miriam Goderich.

Of course, I have an emergency. I'm running out of comments on rejections.

I'm at an offsite today and not on email.
If you need something urgently please be in
touch with Tess Brown at tess@thompsonliter-
ary.com.

Thank you!
--
Meg Thompson / Founder
she / her
Thompson Literary Agency
ph: 347-281-7961
meg@thompsonliterary.com
www.thompsonliterary.com
*please note that we have moved to
48 Great Jones St., Suite #5F,
New York, NY 10012; we are
not in the office Friday-Sunday*

This digital detox thing is very toxic!
If you work with people — do work with
them, in the office or not. I don't care
if you reply to my email from the subway
or your desk or your toilet seat. Which,
by the way, is the only multitasking
one can do: poop and use a cellphone.

Automatic reply from brent@triadaus.com:

I am away from email until the morning of Tuesday, 2/14. Thank you for your patience.

Alrighty, I'll send you a love letter within 8 to 52 weeks.

The agents of Spencerhill Associates are now only accepting unsolicited submissions through their submission portals. Please visit https://www.spencerhillassociates.com/submissions to get the links.

I wish there were a portal where things would work out for once. C'mon, Universe! I want a beach house!

I have struck out on my own and launched Book Wyrm Literary Agency. I want to thank Lori Perkins for her guidance over the past twelve years and continued support for my new venture.

My new email address is sandy@bookwyrmlit.com. I retain my client list from L. Perkins.

If you would like to query me, please check out my submissions guidelines at http://bookwyrmlit.com/submissions.

For L. Perkins related business, please contact Lori at lperkinsagency@yahoo.com.

Best,
Sandy Lu

An automated response from the new business entity name? This changes everything!

Automatic reply from samuel@blakefriedmann.-co.uk:

I have now left Blake Friedmann and publishing. For queries relating to my former clients, please check their author page on the Blake Friedmann website and contact their current agent.

For finance matters,
please contact accounts@blakefriedmann.co.uk

They are now leaving the industry? Eh, maybe they should, indeed.

Thank you so much for choosing to send your submission to us. We dedicate a lot of time to reading and considering every submission we receive, and we love discovering and championing first time authors.

We do understand the time and effort that goes into crafting a submission, and we would like to be able to respond individually to everyone, but due to the sheer volume of submissions we receive on a daily basis we are unable to guarantee a further reply unless we want to read or hear more.

If you don't hear anything from us within eight weeks, please assume your work is not the right fit for our agency. Thank you again for choosing to submit to Janklow & Nesbit UK.

This is an automatically generated email. If you have further questions, please email us at queries@janklow.co.uk and we will be happy to help you.

There are only 3 truly important things on Earth: nature, love, and a sense of humor. Nature helps to live, love to survive, and a sense of humor to live through.

EVERYONE HAS A STORY.
AND IT'S UNIQUE.

"One day I'll write a book…"
No time? Hire a ghostwriter.

MEMOIR. NON-FICTION. ETC.

Keep memories. Share experience. Etc.

- Story development and writing
- Editing
- Layout and cover design
- Printing
- Presentation

A book of 200 pages in 100 days.

"

All good books are alike - after you are finished reading one you will feel that all that happened to you and afterwards it all belongs to you: the good and the bad, the ecstasy, the remorse and sorrow, the people and the places and how the weather was.
~ Ernest Hemingway

MILA ILKOVA
milailkova@proton.me
+1(917)719-0794

www.ingramcontent.com/pod-product-compliance
Lightning Source LLC
Chambersburg PA
CBHW051418090426
42737CB00014B/2731